Tucholsky Wagner Zola Scott Sydow Fonatne Freud Schlegel
Turgenev Wallace
Twain Walther von der Vogelweide Fouqué Friedrich II. von Preußen
Weber Freiligrath Frey
Fechner Fichte Weiße Rose von Fallersleben Kant Ernst Richthofen Frommel
Engels Fielding Hölderlin
Fehrs Faber Flaubert Eichendorff Tacitus Dumas
Maximilian I. von Habsburg Fock Eliasberg Zweig Ebner Eschenbach
Feuerbach Ewald Eliot Vergil
Goethe Elisabeth von Österreich London
Mendelssohn Balzac Shakespeare Dostojewski Ganghofer
Trackl Stevenson Lichtenberg Rathenau Doyle Gjellerup
Mommsen Tolstoi Hambruch Droste-Hülshoff
Thoma Lenz Hanrieder
Dach Verne von Arnim Hägele Hauff Humboldt
Karrillon Reuter Rousseau Hagen Hauptmann Gautier
Garschin Defoe Baudelaire
Damaschke Hebbel
Descartes Hegel Kussmaul Herder
Wolfram von Eschenbach Dickens Schopenhauer Rilke George
Bronner Darwin Melville Grimm Jerome Bebel Proust
Campe Horváth Aristoteles Voltaire Federer
Bismarck Vigny Barlach Heine Herodot
Gengenbach
Storm Casanova Tersteegen Grillparzer Georgy
Chamberlain Lessing Langbein Gilm Gryphius
Brentano Lafontaine
Strachwitz Claudius Schiller Kralik Iffland Sokrates
Katharina II. von Rußland Bellamy Schilling
Gerstäcker Raabe Gibbon Tschechow
Löns Hesse Hoffmann Gogol Wilde Vulpius
Luther Heym Hofmannsthal Gleim
Roth Klee Hölty Morgenstern Goedicke
Luxemburg Heyse Klopstock Kleist
Puschkin Homer Mörike
Machiavelli La Roche Horaz Musil
Navarra Aurel Musset Kierkegaard Kraft Kraus
Lamprecht Kind Kirchhoff Hugo Moltke
Nestroy Marie de France
Laotse Ipsen Liebknecht
Nietzsche Nansen Ringelnatz
Marx Lassalle Gorki Klett Leibniz
von Ossietzky May vom Stein Lawrence Irving
Petalozzi Knigge
Platon Pückler Michelangelo Kock Kafka
Sachs Poe Liebermann
de Sade Praetorius Mistral Zetkin Korolenko

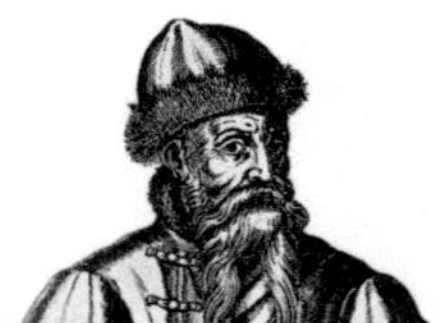

The publishing house tredition has created the series **TREDITION CLASSICS**. It contains classical literature works from over two thousand years. Most of these titles have been out of print and off the bookstore shelves for decades.

The book series is intended to preserve the cultural legacy and to promote the timeless works of classical literature. As a reader of a **TREDITION CLASSICS** book, the reader supports the mission to save many of the amazing works of world literature from oblivion.

The symbol of **TREDITION CLASSICS** is Johannes Gutenberg (1400 – 1468), the inventor of movable type printing.

With the series, tredition intends to make thousands of international literature classics available in printed format again – worldwide.

All books are available at book retailers worldwide in paperback and in hardcover. For more information please visit: www.tredition.com

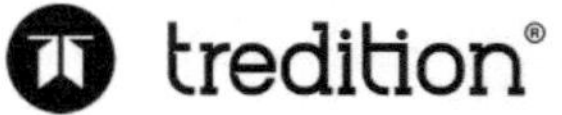

tredition was established in 2006 by Sandra Latusseck and Soenke Schulz. Based in Hamburg, Germany, tredition offers publishing solutions to authors and publishing houses, combined with worldwide distribution of printed and digital book content. tredition is uniquely positioned to enable authors and publishing houses to create books on their own terms and without conventional manufacturing risks.

For more information please visit: www.tredition.com

Bell's Cathedrals: The Cathedral Church of Carlisle A Description of Its Fabric and A Brief History of the Episcopal See

C. King Eley

Imprint

This book is part of the TREDITION CLASSICS series.

Author: C. King Eley
Cover design: toepferschumann, Berlin (Germany)

Publisher: tredition GmbH, Hamburg (Germany)
ISBN: 978-3-8495-0688-9

www.tredition.com
www.tredition.de

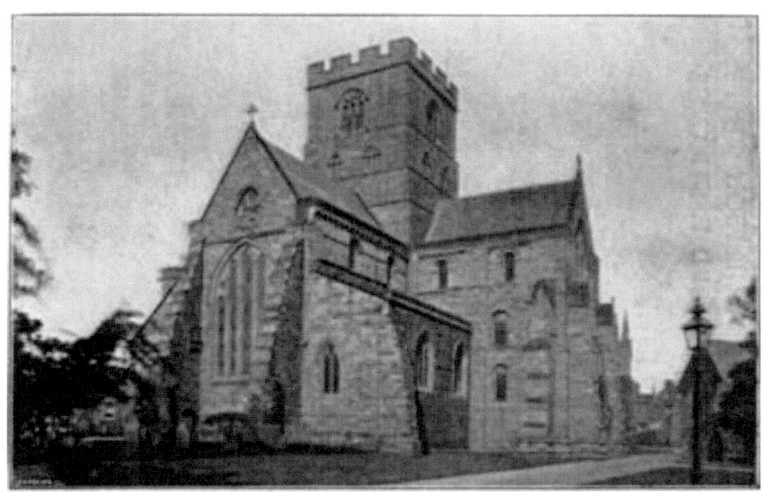

CARLISLE CATHEDRAL FROM THE SOUTH-WEST.

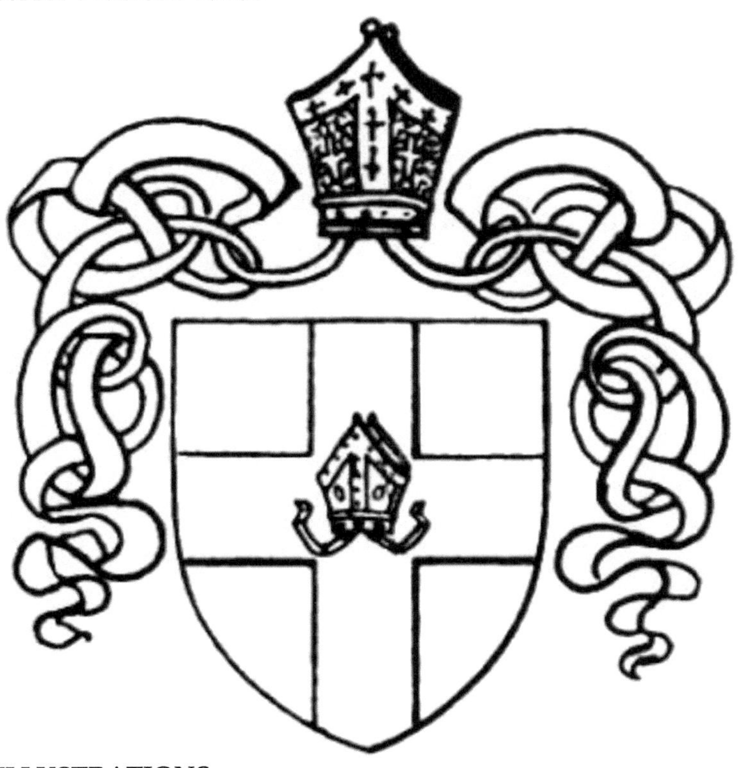

ILLUSTRATIONS

GENERAL PREFACE

This series of monographs has been planned to supply visitors to the great English Cathedrals with accurate and well illustrated guide-books at a popular price. The aim of each writer has been to produce a work compiled with sufficient knowledge and scholarship to be of value to the student of Archæeology and History, and yet not too technical in language for the use of an ordinary visitor or tourist.

To specify all the authorities which have been made use of in each case would be difficult and tedious in this place. But amongst the general sources of information which have been almost invariably found useful are: — (1) the great county histories, the value of which, especially in questions of genealogy and local records, is generally recognised; (2) the numerous papers by experts which appear from time to time in the Transactions of the Antiquarian and Archæological Societies; (3) the important documents made accessible in the series issued by the Master of the Rolls; (4) the well-known works of Britton and Willis on the English Cathedrals; and (5) the excellent series of Handbooks to the Cathedrals originated by the late Mr. John Murray; to which the reader may in most cases be referred for further detail, especially in reference to the histories of the respective sees.

Gleeson White.
Edward F. Strange.

AUTHOR'S PREFACE

Amongst the works consulted in compiling this handbook may be specially mentioned Nicolson and Burn's "History and Antiquities of Westmoreland and Cumberland," Hutchinson's "History and Antiquities of the City of Carlisle," Jefferson's "History and Antiquities of Carlisle," Billings' "Architectural Illustrations, History and Description of Carlisle Cathedral," "Guide to the Cathedral, Carlisle," by R.H. and K.H.

Much help has also been obtained from the late J.R. Green's historical works, as well as the various biographies in the "National Dictionary of Biography."

I also wish to record my thanks to my friend, Mr. A. Tapley, who kindly read through part of the manuscript; and to Mr. A. Pumphrey for permission to reproduce the photographs used.

C.K.E.

CONTENTS

LIST OF ILLUSTRATIONS

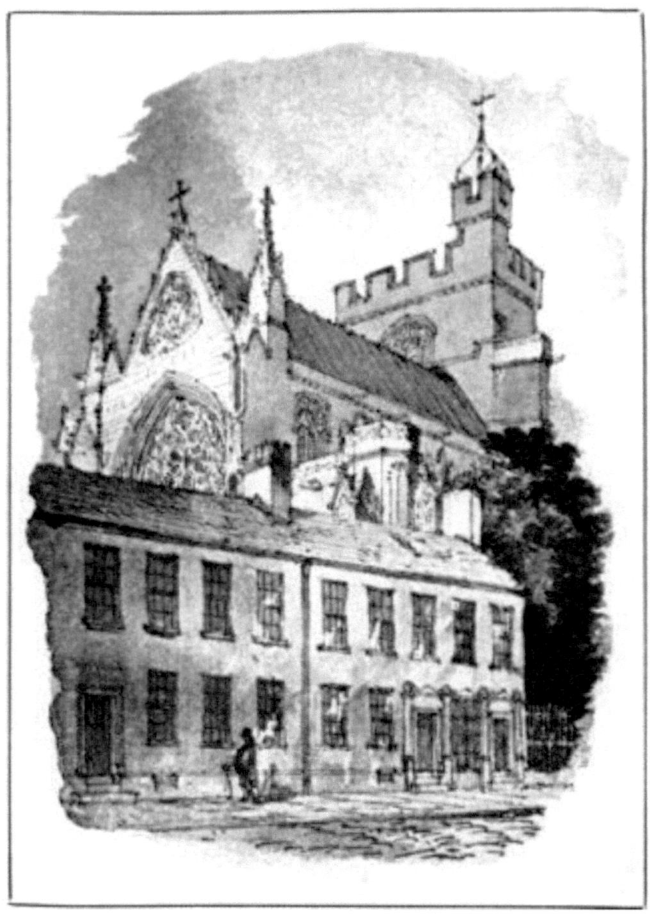

THE CATHEDRAL FROM THE NORTH-EAST.
From an original Drawing by R.W. Billings.
Table of
Contents
3

CARLISLE CATHEDRAL

CHAPTER I

HISTORY OF THE CATHEDRAL CHURCH OF THE HOLY AND UNDIVIDED TRINITY

The details of the founding of the cathedral of Carlisle are very precise and clear.

When William Rufus returned southwards after re-establishing the city of Carlisle, he left as governor a rich Norman priest named Walter. He began at once to build a church to be dedicated to the Blessed Virgin Mary, which was to have in connection with it a college of secular canons. Walter did not, however, live to see the building finished, and Henry I. took it upon himself to complete the good work. It is said that his wife on one hand, and his chaplain on the other, urged him to do this. By the beginning of the twelfth century (1123) he founded and endowed a priory of regular Augustinian canons, making his chaplain the first prior.

Ten years afterwards—1133—Henry founded the see of Carlisle, and the priory church became the cathedral. At its endowment Henry laid on the altar the famous "cornu eburneum," now lost. This horn was given, instead of a written document, as proof of the grants of tithes. Its virtue was tried in 1290 when the prior claimed some tithes on land in the forest of Inglewood, but it was decided that the grant did not originally cover the tithes in dispute. "The ceremony of investiture with a horn is very ancient, and was in use before there were any written charters. We read of Ulf, a Danish prince, who gave all his lands to the church of York; and the form of endowment was this: he brought the horn out of which he usually drank, and before the high altar kneeling devoutly drank the wine, and by that ceremony enfeoffed the church with all his lands and revenues." (Jefferson, "History of Carlisle," 171*n*.)

4 Aldulf (or Æthelwulf) was made the first bishop, and he placed Augustinians in the monastery attached to the cathedral. These were called "black" canons, their cassocks, cloaks, and hoods being of that colour. A further difference between them and other monks

was that they let their beards grow and covered their heads with caps. As a consequence of this order being introduced into the monastery the Episcopal chapter was Augustinian, other English cathedral chapters being generally Benedictine.

On some high ground between the west wall of the city, and the road to the castle the cathedral was built. The site was nearly square in shape, about five acres in extent, and was the highest part in Carlisle after that on which the castle stood. This situation was very advantageous owing to the presence of water near the surface, its frontage to the city wall, and proximity to the river. A narrow piece of ground of about half-an-acre, extending along the walls, and upon which the monastic grounds abutted, was in after years given to the priory by its owner, Robert de Eglesfield, who was chaplain to Philippa, wife of Henry III.

The church was set out, almost due east and west, diagonally across the north-west part of the site, the west end being about 100 feet from the boundary; and was finished about 1130. Its nave consisted of eight bays, and was about 140 feet long.

There was a very fine west front with a handsome central doorway of four orders. The western wall was more than 7 feet in thickness, and had four flat pilaster buttresses nearly 7 feet broad, and 15 inches deep.

The nave was provided with north and south aisles covered with high-pitched wooden roofs, while the north and south transepts were also roofed in a similar manner, and a small apsidal chapel projected from the eastern face of each. The archway of the south transept apse is now the entrance to St. Catherine's Chapel. With the exception of the present elaborate entrance to the south transept and the window above it, the transept is identical with that of the Norman minster.

The choir was only 80 feet long, reaching to the end of the present stalls. Eastward it terminated in an apse. Its width can be judged from traces of the original roof, still perceptible in the west wall of the present choir. In accordance with a frequent arrangement, the ritual choir extended westward of 5 the crossing, and included the two eastern bays of the nave.

In the centre was a low square typical Norman tower, 35 feet square, of which the lower parts of the piers remain. To allow for the extension of the ritual choir the eastern and western arches of the crossing were carried on corbels.

White or grey sandstone from quarries in the district was used in the construction of the minster, perhaps supplemented by stones from the Roman wall. Stucco was applied to the exterior, red lines marking the joints. There is no doubt that this stucco has materially helped to keep the Norman stone-work in a good state of preservation.

It will be seen then that the original church was a Norman minster, of moderate size, consisting of a nave, with north and south aisles, a small choir, a low square tower, and north and south transepts.

Thus it remained till about 1250, when, as usually happened, the clergy became dissatisfied with the smallness of their choir, and a new one was projected on a much larger scale. Its length was to be equal to the nave, while in height and breadth it was to be greater. The increased length allowed room for the ritual choir on the east side of the crossing.

Any extension of the cathedral on the south was prevented by the presence of the conventual buildings: therefore the north choir-aisle was thrown into the choir, and a new one added northward of the former. One consequence of this alteration is seen by comparing the entrance to each aisle. That of the south choir aisle is the original Norman arch, while the entrance to the north aisle is a beautiful late thirteenth-century arch (Decorated). The corresponding Norman arch of the north aisle has been blocked up, but is still easily traced.

Another consequence is, that the extension having taken place on one side only, the eastern arch of the tower fills but a part of the west end of the choir. The choir arch consequently is symmetrically placed with regard to the roof of the nave, but not with the choir roof; and the central line of the choir does not coincide with that of the nave; for, though the south wall of the choir is in a line with the south wall of the nave, the choir being 12 feet broader than the nave, the axis of the former is to the north of the axis of the nave.

The view from 6 the east end looking towards the nave is quite spoiled by this want of symmetry.

Not very much remains to-day of this thirteenth-century Early English choir. In 1292, just as it had been roofed in, a terrible fire, the most disastrous the cathedral has ever experienced, destroyed everything except the outer walls of the aisles, the graceful lancet windows, and the beautiful cinque-foiled arcading beneath them. Belfry and bells, too, shared in the destruction.

One hundred years passed away while a new choir was being built. Bishop Halton (1292-1325), a very energetic prelate, and a great favourite of Edward I., began the work, and laboured at it for quite thirty years, and was followed by Bishops Kirkby, Welton, and Appleby. It was arranged to rebuild the choir on a still larger scale, a bay being added, and the east end rebuilt from the foundation. The general plan of the earlier work of the aisles was followed in the new bay. The glory of the cathedral—the great east window, which marks a distinct transition in art—was also projected, but at this time only carried up as high as the top of the choir arches.

The wall arcade and the lancet windows above were repaired, and later work of a more elaborate character added. The great arches, and the groin ribs of the aisle ceilings were underset with new pillars; so that we get Early English *arches* of the thirteenth century on Decorated *pillars* of the fourteenth century.

After some years interval, building was resumed about 1350. The Decorated portions of the choir were now put in hand: the triforium, clerestory, and upper part of the east end, as well as the tracery and much of the mouldings of the east window and the roof. The carving, hitherto unfinished, was now completed; but, as the style had developed in the mean-time, we once more find examples of decidedly early work with much later work both above and below. The roof inside was finished with a very fine panelled ceiling. The building was finished 1375-1400, and in the roof were placed the arms of those who had helped in the rebuilding—the Lacys, the Nevilles, and the Percys.

The material used for the new choir was red sandstone, both for the interior and the exterior, giving in some cases a curious patched appearance to the walls.7

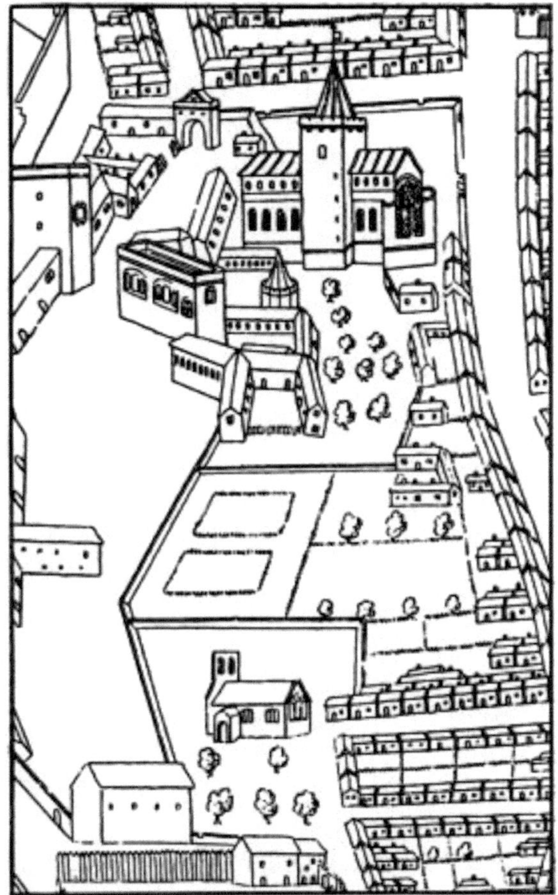

THE CATHEDRAL AND PRECINCTS.
From an old Plan in Lyson's "Magna Britannia."

8 About 1380-1384 the east window was filled with glass.

In 1392 the cathedral once again suffered from fire, and the damage was repaired by Bishop Strickland (1400-19). No efforts appear to have been made to bring the nave into correspondence with the extended choir, and the end of the thirteenth century marks the close of the cathedral's history in the direction of its enlargement and beautifying.

On a review of the cathedral we find in the aisles thirteenth-century work, on a small scale, in its perfection.

The south aisle shows development of window tracery, and the gradual steps taken towards uniting single lights under one arch.

Tracery carried to its perfection can be seen in the east window.

Early English carving is shown in St. Catherine's Chapel, especially in the corbels; and the more naturalistic carving which was developed at a later period, is exhibited in the corbels of the roof of the choir and the capitals of the piers. The latter afford the most complete representation of the seasons known to exist. On the south side (from east to west) are the first six months, and on the north side (west to east) the remainder.

About 1401, William Strickland being Bishop of Carlisle, the tower was rebuilt on its original scale, probably because the foundations would not permit one to be erected proportioned to the size of the choir. It was capped by a short wooden spire covered with lead; this, however, was removed in the seventeenth century.

The forty-six stalls in the choir, erected on a plinth of red sandstone, belong to this period (1401-19). The elaborate tabernacle work by Prior Haithwaite (1433) was originally gilded and coloured, and the niches were filled with images.

Prior Gondibour (1484-1507) painted the backs of the stalls. The remains of some screens he added to the choir may still be seen in St. Catherine's Chapel.

He had the roof painted in red, green, and gold, on a white ground; painted the choir pillars white, diapered with red roses nearly 12 inches in diameter, and with the letters I.H.C. and J.M. in gold; and no doubt finished whatever decorative work of the choir still had to be done.

Laurence Salkeld, last prior, and first dean, erected the 9 very fine Renaissance screen on the north side of the choir, near the pulpit. It bears his initials, followed by the letters D.K. (*Decanus Karliolensis*), of his new title.

The priory was surrendered to the Crown in January 1540, and the last prior—Salkeld—was made dean of the chapter founded by

Henry VIII. The revenue was at that time estimated at £481 per annum. Five years later, June 1545, the present foundation was settled, and the dedication changed to that of the Holy and Undivided Trinity.

We get a glimpse of the cathedral in the first half of the seventeenth century, in the record left by some officers who visited the English cathedrals in 1634. Carlisle they curtly speak of as "more like a great wilde country church" than a fair and stately cathedral.

After the capture of the city in 1645 the parliamentary troops pulled down part of the nave in order to repair the fortifications. It is very probable that the Norman church was partly built of stones taken from the Roman wall; and it is strange to find the western part of the same church being destroyed nearly six hundred years after in order to repair the city walls.

George Fox, the intrepid founder of the Society of Friends, came to Carlisle in 1653 and preached in the cathedral. Some of the congregation being opposed to him, he was guarded while preaching, by certain soldiers and friends who had "heard him gladly." At length the "rude people of the city" rushed into the building, and made a tumult, so that the governor was forced to send musketeers to quell it.

Fox thus describes the scene, in his "Journal":

"From thence we came to Carlisle.

"On the First-day following I went into the steeple-house: and after the priest had done, I preached the truth to the people, and declared the word of life amongst them. The priest got away, and the magistrates desired me to go out of the steeple-house. But I still declared the way of the Lord unto them, and told them, 'I came to speak the word of life and salvation from the Lord amongst them.' The power of the Lord was dreadful amongst them in the steeple-house, so that the people trembled and shook, and they thought the steeple-house shook: and some of them feared it would fall down on their heads. The magistrates' wives were in a rage and strove mightily to be at me: but the soldiers and friendly people 10 stood thick about me. At length the rude people of the city rose, and came with staves and stones into the steeple-house crying, 'Down with these round-headed rogues'; and they threw stones. Whereupon the governor sent a file or two of musketeers into the steeple-house, to appease the tumult, and commanded all the other soldiers out. So those soldiers took me by the hand in a friendly manner, and said they would have me along with them. When we came forth into the street, the city was in an uproar, and the governor came down; and some of those soldiers were put in prison for standing by me, and for me, against the town's-people.

"The next day the justices and magistrates of the town granted a warrant against me and sent for me to come before them. After a large examination they committed me to prison as a blasphemer, a heretic, and a seducer: though they could not justly charge any such thing against me."

Fuller, about 1660, describes the building as "black but comely, still bearing the remaining signes of its former burning."

Further mischief was also done to the building by the Jacobite prisoners who were lodged in it after the defeat of the Young Pretender.

In the latter half of the eighteenth century some attempts were made at restoring the cathedral, but they for the most part consisted of hiding the beautiful choir roof with a stucco groined ceiling, and plentifully whitewashing the building.

"The roof was 'elegantly' vaulted with wood. But this failing by length of time, together with the lead roof, the dean and chapter some few years ago new laid the roof, and the ceiling being totally ruined and destroyed they in the year 1764 contracted for a stucco groined ceiling, and for cleaning and whitening the whole church. And finding the new lead much torn and broken by wind for want of a ceiling underneath, the upper tire of that was done again, and a coping added to the rigging. And thus proceeding from one repair to another the whole expence hath amounted to upwards of £1300."[1]

Eastward of the stalls the choir was formerly separated from the aisles by screens of elaborate tracery work. When the cathedral was "repaired and beautified" as just described, they were removed to outbuildings, and by far the greater part lost or destroyed.

11 The cathedral was restored 1853-7, in good taste, at a cost of about £15,000. Mr. Ewan Christian, the architect of the Ecclesiastical Commissioners, undertook the work, and happily succeeded in counteracting the "repairing and beautifying" of 1764.

Carlisle is not a large or notable cathedral, but its delightful Early English choir with its magnificent east window will ever redeem it from being insignificant or uninteresting.

CHAPTER II

THE EXTERIOR

On examining the north side of the cathedral, it is apparent that more than one plan has been followed in the construction of the building as it stands.

There are the remains of a Norman nave whose roof is lower than the choir roof. The choir is Early English with clerestory windows, and the easternmost bay (the retro-choir) Late Decorated; while the tower is Perpendicular. In the north window of the north transept we have a specimen of work of the nineteenth century. Thus the cathedral supplies examples of architecture from the Norman period down to the present time.

The moderate height of the **Nave** (65 ft.), and the treatment of its details, are quite characteristic of the best work of the period when it was erected.

The bays of the aisle are separated by flat buttresses about five and a half feet wide projecting nearly one foot beyond the wall, and the parapet wall in which they terminate is supported above the windows by a corbel table of shields and trefoil heads.[2]

Upon the string-course which runs along the wall unbroken by the buttresses there is in each bay a window with a circular head, flanked by single columns. A ring-like ornament is used as a decoration for one of the mouldings of the arch.

These windows, except the one above the doorway, are restorations. The doorway itself, which leads into the nave, is modern, imitated from the Norman window.

The Clerestory in each compartment has a window which differs from the aisle windows in having the billet as decoration of its outer moulding. The string-course at the spring of the round head runs without a break from one to the other.

There is also an unbroken corbel table above the windows, of very expressive, life-like heads, no two of which are alike. 13

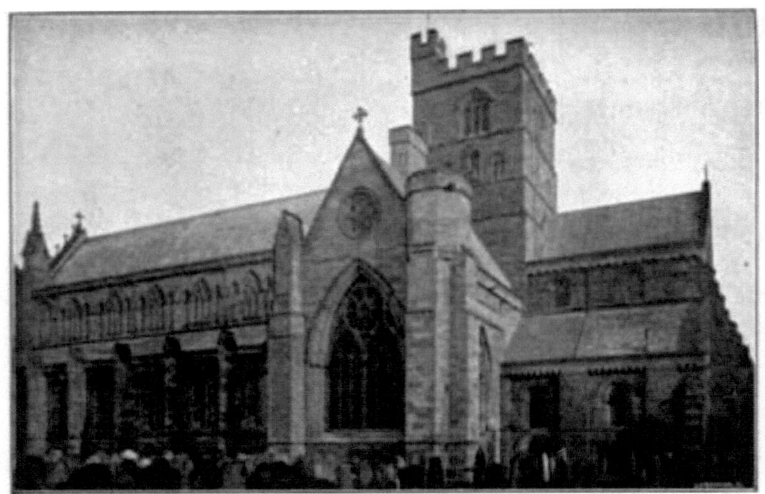

THE CATHEDRAL FROM THE NORTH.

15North Transept.—The north window is Debased Gothic, the tracery of the previous window having been similar to that of the great east window, while the west window is early English.

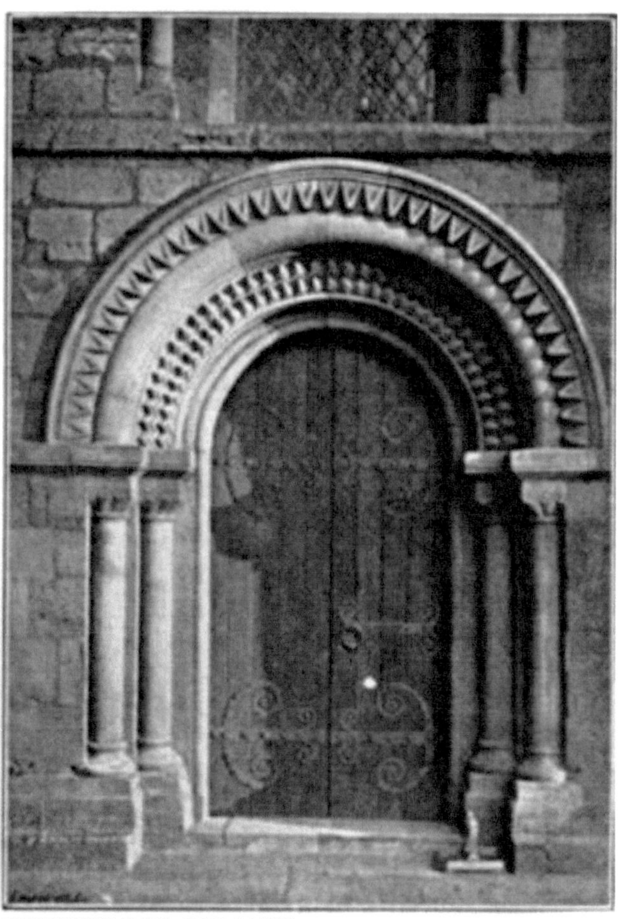

NORTH DOOR OF NAVE.

The **Tower**, the latest part of the cathedral, was the work of Bishop Strickland early in the fifteenth century. He erected it upon the piers of the ancient Norman tower. Its height is not much over 100 feet, and is very disappointing, because in England "cathedral towers are apt to be good, and really make 16 their mark" (Pater). In fact, it does not at all give the impression of being part of such an important building as a cathedral. This is caused by its having been rebuilt on the scale of the Norman nave, and not on that of the enlarged choir. It takes up only about two-thirds of the width of the choir, and to mask this defect a turret rising to the top of the third stage of the tower is introduced on the north side, and another turret is added at the north-east angle.

The tower rises in four stages above the transepts. The second storey is pierced with loopholes. The third has two pointed windows lighting a room immediately below the belfry. Between these, in a niche with a canopy, is the figure of an angel holding a drawn sword. On his head is fixed a tablet to support another figure. There is only one window in the fourth storey, which gives light to the belfry, and is very large. Its labels are ornamented with very vigorously carved heads, and the cornice above is decorated very much like that of the clerestory. The tower terminates in an embattled parapet.

All the windows have been thrown out of centre by the addition of the lower turret.

Originally the tower was crowned by a leaden spire about fifteen feet in height, but this was removed at the end of the seventeenth century on account of its decayed condition.

On the east side of the tower there is a single window in the third storey. In place of a second window there is an opening into the roof of the choir. This leads into a passage running from the tower to the east end.

The bold attempts to veil the inadequate size of the tower by the addition of two turrets can be best studied from this side.

The North Aisle of the **Choir** consists of eight bays, all Early English, except the easternmost one (the retro-choir), which is Late Decorated; while the western bay has a Perpendicular window.

Sometime in the fifteenth century the third bay from the east, in each aisle, was altered and a large Perpendicular window inserted in order to admit more light to the sanctuary. During the restoration of the cathedral these later windows were removed, and replaced by careful copies of the other Early English windows.

The basement is composed of bold mouldings with a plain wall equivalent in height to the internal wall arcade. Over 17 this, a string-course runs uninterruptedly round the choir just below the windows.

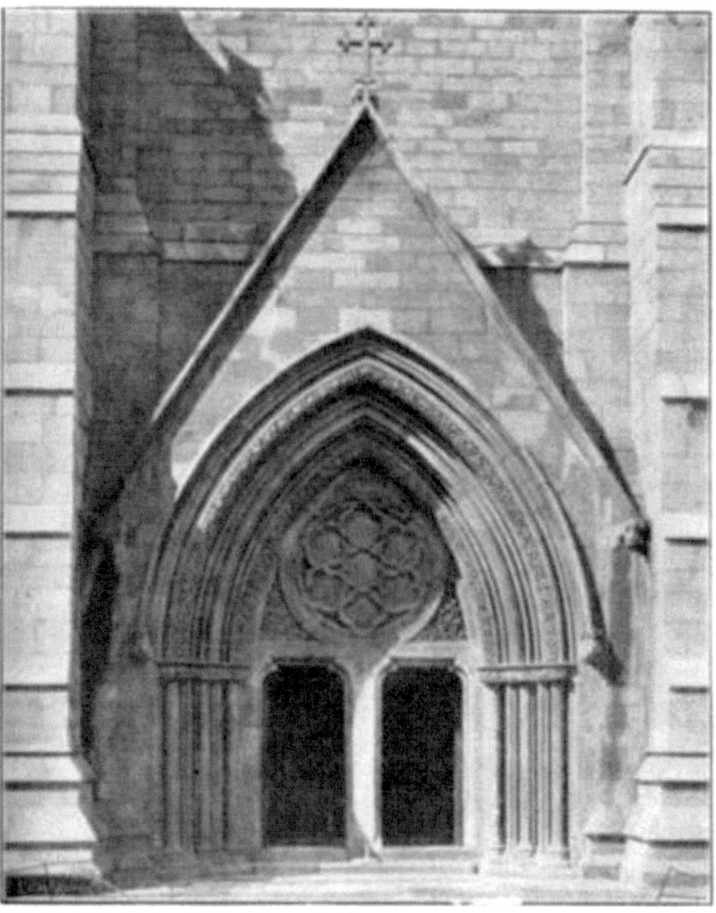

THE SOUTH DOOR. (See p. 21.)

Each compartment has an arcade of four lancet-shaped divisions, the external ones blank; while the internal divisions (which are wider than the others) form the window. The 18 slender, banded, shafts are detached, which is rather unusual, and have moulded bases and capitals. The bands divide the shafts into unequal lengths, the lower portion being the shorter. The arch mouldings are good. Owing to

31

the fact that the blank arches are more acutely pointed, their outer mouldings terminate higher than the mouldings of the internal arches.

Towards the east end small heads, and bosses of foliage, ornament the junction of these mouldings. Above these the cornice and parapet rest upon blocks bearing the nail-head ornament.

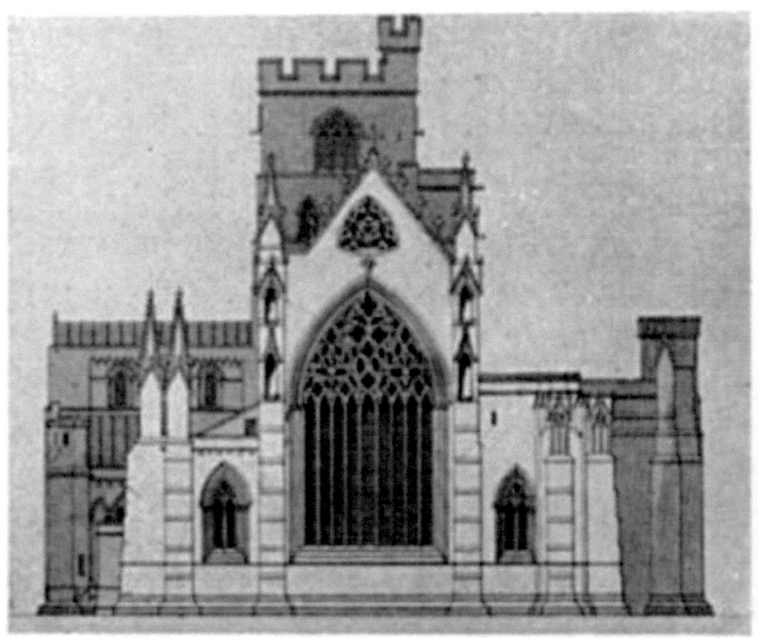

ELEVATION OF EAST END.

The second bay from the east is divided into three equal spaces, with a very narrow acute angle on the right.

A series of fine gabled buttresses gives relief to the exterior of the choir on each side.

The windows of the **Clerestory** have very rich mouldings, and also afford fine examples of flowing tracery. Each bay has an arch with three divisions, the central one higher and wider 19 than the others. On this side only — the north — the base is ornamented with trefoils.

There is a cornice above the windows extending from the tower to the east end. It is richly decorated with heads and the ball-flower ornament which is characteristic of fourteenth-century work. It is broken here and there by gargoyles projecting almost three feet from the wall. The parapet makes but a poor show in comparison with the rich windows and cornice.

As the choir never had a groined ceiling there was no necessity for flying buttresses, and their absence gives the clerestory a very monotonous flat effect. This is further intensified by the window tracery being level with the wall, the architraves having no depth of moulding round them.

Some years ago the aisles and clerestory were skilfully refaced, and consequently the exteriors have a very modern appearance.

East of the retro-choir is the exterior of a staircase leading from the north choir aisle to the clerestory parapet. It terminates in a highly-finished octagonal turret whose parapet is enriched with a running trefoil ornament resembling that on the base of the clerestory windows. The north-eastern and the small east buttresses terminate just beneath, in gables richly ornamented with minute crockets. The panelling of the former is rather like the decoration of the central portion of the east end.

East End.—An irregularity in designing the east end has been covered by placing the great buttresses so as to make the pediment appear irregular, and the cross at the apex seems, consequently, not to be in the centre of the choir; while, in fact, it is the great east window (with the gable window over it) that is out of position.

The sill of the east window is unusually near the ground, and it is flanked by substantial buttresses finely pinnacled. Each buttress contains two niches with beautifully carved canopies: the base of the lower ones being a trifle higher than the springing of the arch. They display full-length statues of St. Peter, St. Paul, St. James, and St. John.

A staircase crossing over the east window in the thickness of the wall receives light from the triangular window enclosing three trefoils which appears in the gable. Immediately beneath this Trinity window — as it is called — is a richly-canopied niche adorned with a statue of the Virgin Mary bearing in her arms the Holy Child.

20 The summit of the gable is crowned by a large richly-floriated cross; and on each side are four smaller ones, with crockets of foliage between them.

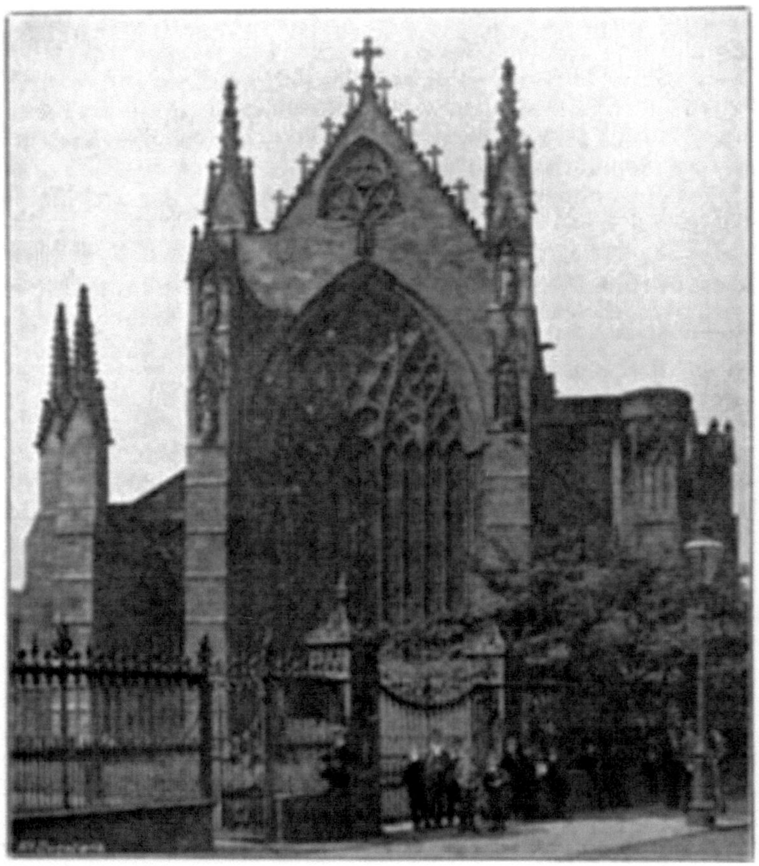

THE EAST END.

In spite of the fact that the east end has been almost entirely rebuilt, it is a remarkably good example of Late Decorated work, and it would be difficult to find its equal in England.

The wall of the north aisle is higher than the south aisle, because of a passage between the staircases. The buttresses 21 do not rise above the parapet, and are finished off with richly-panelled gables, ornamented with crockets and finials.

The end of the south aisle is decorated with corbels and parapet, like the choir, and with pinnacled buttresses.

On the south side of the **Choir** the first three bays from the east end are practically the same as those on the north side.

The remaining windows, including those of St. Catherine's Chapel on the east of the south transept, are Early English, but of later date and not so pleasing as the others. Instead of two lights they are furnished with three; some of these have small circular openings in the spandrels over the mullions filled with stained glass.

The fifth compartment (against which a vestry was formerly built) shows traces of a door, and over that a passage, probably connected originally with some of the conventual buildings.

The grotesque gargoyles, "these wild faces, these images of beasts and men carved upon spouts and gutters," are very vigorously executed.

The windows on the south side of the clerestory are without the trefoil which ornaments the base of those on the north side.

The blank window next to the tower is also wanting; in other respects the clerestory presents the same features as on the north.

South Transept.—The chapter-house and cloisters formerly adjoined the south transept, and there was probably an entrance from the chapter-house leading down a flight of stairs into the transept. Billings says: "The modern casing at the base of the end of the transept (about 12 ft. high) shews the height of the **Cloisters**: and the doorway above, the level of the chapter-house floor. From this it would seem that the cathedral was entered at the south transept from the chapter-house by a flight of steps."

The foundation of the south wall having been shaken by the removal of the remains of the conventual buildings, massive buttresses were added, and a very richly sculptured doorway inserted between them (1856). It was designed by Mr. Christian and is the principal entrance to the Cathedral. Its character is that of the late work of the choir, and is somewhat out of keeping with this distinctively Norman portion of the building.

The window over the entrance is of the same date.

22 The west side of the transept is lighted by two plain round-headed windows, not quite central.

The outer moulding of the window arch of the south transept clerestory has billet ornament. Above this is a corbel table of heads and mouldings which interferes with the upper window mouldings. The transept compartments differ from those of the nave by the addition of a flat buttress between each, which consequently breaks the continuity of the corbel table.

As the side of the nave was covered by the conventual buildings it was of plainer character than the north, and had no buttresses between the windows.

The clerestory is exactly the same as on the north.

The foundations of the old west wall are behind one of the prebendary's houses to the west of the nave.

The west end, as it stands at present, was restored by Mr. Christian.

A local sandstone was used in the construction of the building: grey, or white in the Norman portion, and red in the other parts. This red sandstone is not so good for exterior as for interior work, because it is liable to perish by the action of the weather.24

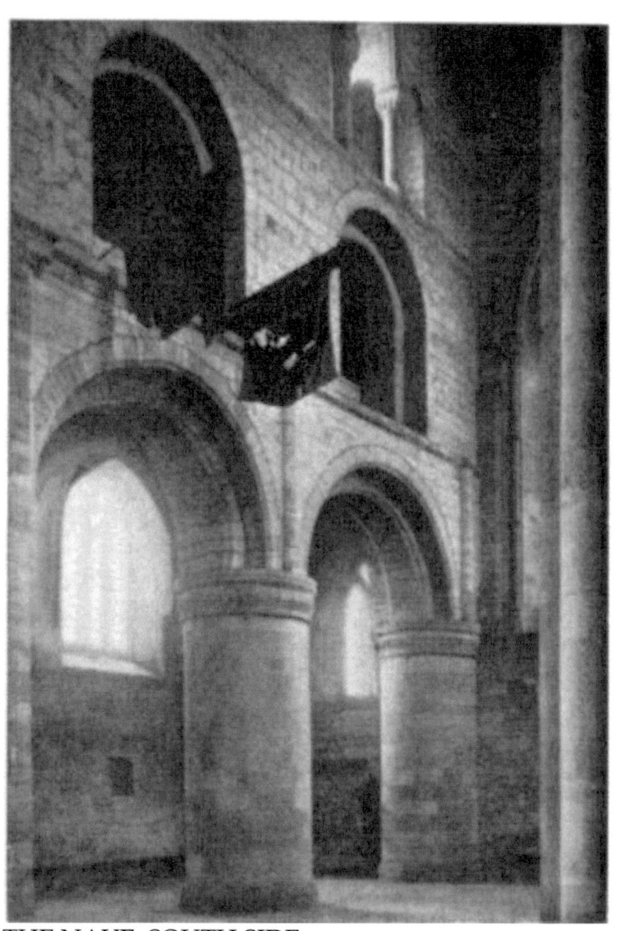

THE NAVE, SOUTH SIDE.

CHAPTER III

THE INTERIOR

The cathedral now consists of part of the original nave (the two eastern bays only) with aisles; and north and south transepts without aisles, but with a chapel on the east side of the south transept; the central tower; and the choir with north and south aisles and ambulatory or retro-choir.

The **Nave.**—Entering by the modern doorway on the north, we are at once in the fragmentary nave, of Early Norman work. Its present length is about 38 feet and width about 60 feet. In 1645 the Scots destroyed about 100 feet of the nave, and it has never been rebuilt. This mutilation has had a serious effect upon the proportions of the building, and induces a feeling of want of balance. The open timber roof, raised to the original height, was substituted at the restoration for a flat ceiling which had been put up at a previous "embellishment" of the cathedral. Bishop Walkelin made use of similar roofs in Winchester Cathedral (1070-1097).

The triforium (1140-50) has in each compartment a semi-circular arch entirely without ornament.

The clerestory consists of three arches supported by columns with carved capitals; the centre arch, which is larger than the other, is lighted at the back by a round-headed window.

We may say that the nave is

"propped

With pillars of prodigious girth."

They are massive circular columns nearly six feet in diameter, and support semi-circular arches. The capitals of those on the south side are carved with leaf ornament; the rest are plain. Against the wall between each arch is a semi-circular engaged shaft reaching to the base of the triforium. The arches near the tower have been partly crushed owing to the shifting of the tower piers caused by faulty foundations. About 1870 the west end of the nave was restored by Mr. Christian. 26 The window is filled with glass, in memory of the

Rev. C. Vernon Harcourt, canon and prebendary of Carlisle (d. 1870).

One of the south aisle windows — the "Soldiers'" window — is in memory of men and officers of the 34th (or Cumberland) [**Transcriber's note: corrected typo, close parentheses] Regiment, who fell in the Crimea, and in India during the mutiny. Three Old Testament warriors appear in stained glass — Joshua, Jerubbaal ("who is Gideon"), and Judas Maccabeus. The battle-torn fragmentary regimental colours hang from the arch opposite. Just beneath this window a doorway (now blocked up) formerly led from the cloisters into the nave.

Up to the year 1870 the nave was used as a parish church. The cathedral from its beginning as the priory church, in accordance with a very common practice of the Augustinian body, contained two churches belonging to two separate bodies quite independent of each other.

The choir and transepts formed the priory church, in the possession of the prior and canons until the dissolution of the monastery, when it passed to the dean and chapter. The nave formed the parish church of St. Mary, and belonged to the parishioners. After the civil wars it was cut off from the transepts by a stone wall, and furnished with galleries and a pulpit. A new church to accommodate the parishioners having been built in the abbey grounds in 1870, all these additions were removed, and the nave was restored to the cathedral, adding greatly to the general effect. An interesting event in the history of the parish church was the marriage of Sir Walter Scott to Miss Carpenter on the 24th December 1797.

He had made the acquaintance of Miss Carpenter at Gilsland in July while touring in the Lake district. She had "a form that was fashioned as light as a fay's, a complexion of the clearest and lightest olive; eyes large, deep-set, and dazzling, of the finest Italian brown; and a profusion of silken tresses black as the raven's wing." Scott was strongly attracted to her, and within six months she became his wife.

A tombstone under the west window shows the matrix of what was once a magnificent brass.

The **Font**, standing on a fine marble flooring close to the west window, has bronze figures of St. John Baptist, the Virgin and Child, and St. Philip. It was designed by Sir A. Blomfield, and presented by Archdeacon Prescott 1891. 27

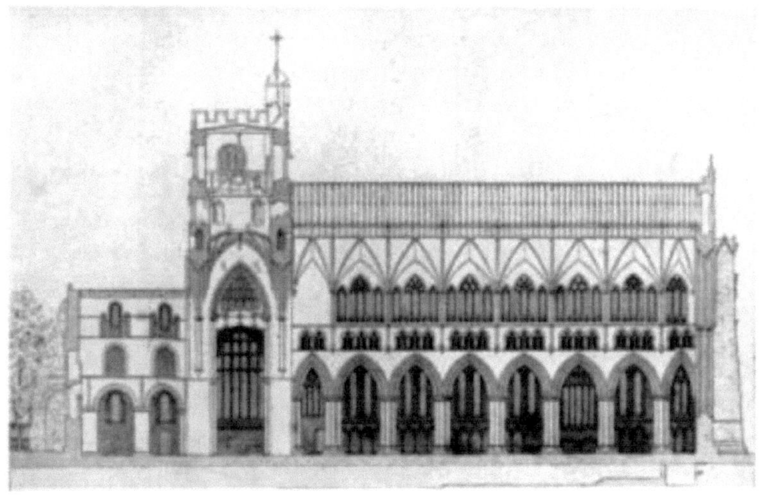

LONGITUDINAL SECTION, NORTH.

28 The **Organ.**—The former organ built by Avery, London, has been given to Hexham Abbey Church. The present one extends from one side of the eastern tower arch to the other. It was built by Willis (1856), and the diaper work was executed by Hardman. About the year 1877 it was enlarged at a cost of nearly £1000.

North Transept.—The transept is very lofty and very dark. It is about 22 feet wide, and its length from north to south is nearly 114 feet.

Standing near the entrance to the north choir aisle, looking southwards and across the nave, a capital general view of the remains of the Norman portion of the cathedral can be obtained.

This end of the transept was rebuilt after the fire of 1292. Having been greatly injured by another fire that broke out about a hundred years later, Bishop Strickland rebuilt it (1400-19.) During the restoration of the cathedral it was once again rebuilt.

On the west side is a Norman arch, the entrance to the north aisle of the nave. The sinking of the tower piers has partly crushed it out of shape. The portion of an arch visible above, acts as a buttress to the tower arches. To the right is a late thirteenth-century window filled with glass in memory of the Rev. Walter Fletcher, Chancellor of Carlisle (died 1846). This window exhibits plate tracery — tracery cut, as it were, out of a flat plate of stone, without mouldings, not built up in sections. It is the transitional link between the lancet and tracery systems.

The doorway in the corner communicates with the transept roof.

The north window is very large, and is filled with stained glass in memory of five children of A.C. Tait, Dean of Carlisle, afterwards Archbishop of Canterbury. They all died of scarlet fever in the short space of five weeks, 6th March to 9th April 1858.

This end of the transept was till quite recently railed off, and used as the consistory court of the Chancellor of Carlisle.

Originally the transept had a chapel on the eastern side opening with a single arch, similar to St. Catherine's Chapel in the south transept.

The opening to the north choir aisle is Decorated in style; above this is a portion of an arch for buttressing the tower-arches.

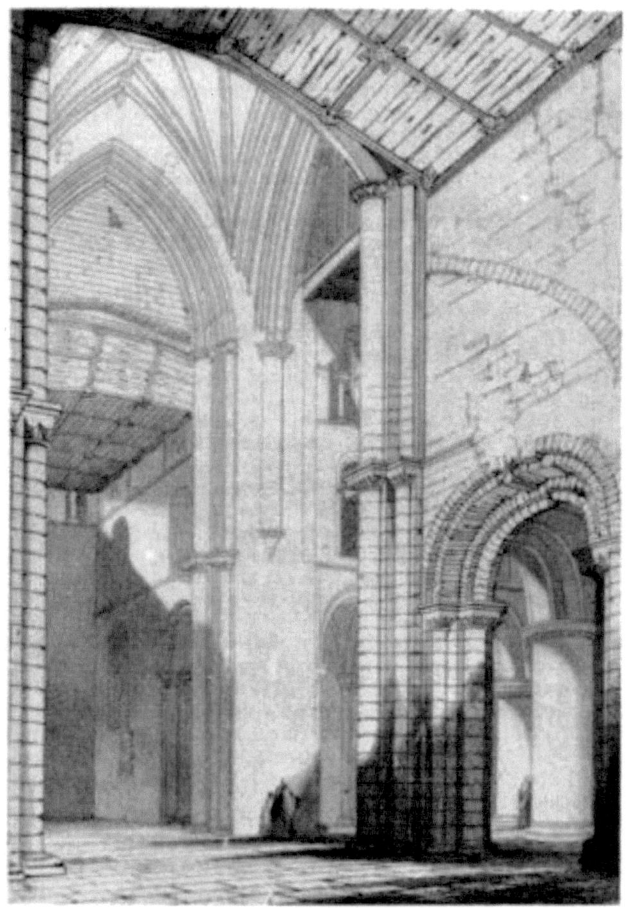

VIEW ACROSS THE TRANSEPTS IN 1840.

30To the right is the blocked-up entrance of the old Norman choir aisle, an exact counterpart of the present south choir aisle entrance.

The roof is now an open timber one of the original pitch.

Near the north-east pier of the tower is a well, completely covered over. This, it is said, was done by a former dean, on the supposition that the well, or the water, in some occult fashion, affected the music in the cathedral.

The **Tower** was rebuilt by Bishop Strickland (1400-19), who used the Norman piers, and placed upon them other columns of about the same length. The Early Norman piers have square-fluted capitals and are a little higher than the arches of the nave. The added columns have capitals carved with birds and foliage, and are carried up to the arches of the tower. This rebuilding was rendered necessary by the shifting of its foundations. The piers sank nearly one foot, and the arches near them have been to some extent distorted. Springs of water are said to run across the transept from north to south, and this may explain the sinking, which probably happened before the erection of the present choir.

Clustered columns uphold the transept arches, but the western and eastern arches are supported on each side by a single column terminating in a bracket at about the level of the base of the triforium. This was arranged so as to increase the width of the passage between the piers from the choir to the nave.

The decoration of the eastern arch capitals consists of the badges of the Percy family — the crescent and fetterlock. Hotspur was Governor of the town and Warden of the Marches under Henry IV., and it is probable that he aided in the work of the bishop. The western arch capitals have, as decoration, the rose and escallop shell alternately — badges of the Dacres and Nevilles, who also may have been benefactors to the cathedral.

Across the north transept from the upper capitals is a depressed arch of stone with Perpendicular tracery.

South Transept. — With the exception of the wall itself, the south arm of the transept is modern. The ancient wall, eight feet thick, is quite suitable for a fortress. A richly-decorated modern doorway has been made, and above it is a window by Powell, representing the "Days of Creation."31

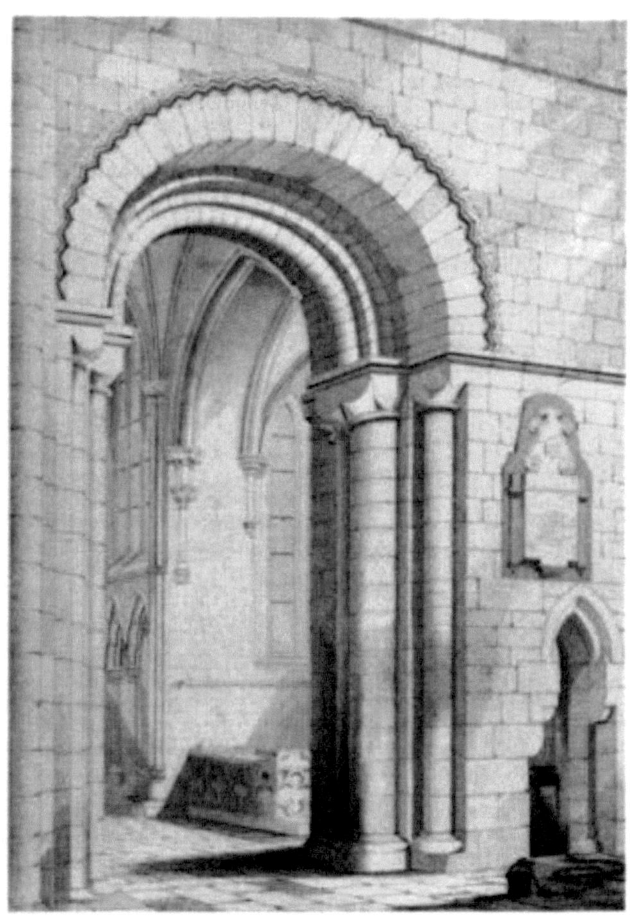

PART OF SOUTH TRANSEPT AND ST. CATHERINE'S CHAPEL.

32The west wall is out of the perpendicular through the shifting of the tower piers, and the Norman arch, opening to the south aisle of the nave has also been distorted. To the left is a round-headed window, filled with glass in memory of the Rev. W. Vansittart, canon and prebendary of Carlisle 1824.

The triforium has a plain rounded opening.

The clerestory is very much like that of the nave, but is not so regular in construction, the architecture being merely massive and destitute of ornament, except in the case of the capitals, which are very sparingly decorated.

On the east side of the transept, the second arch from the doorway, is the entrance to the south choir aisle. It is Norman, ornamented with a simply executed but very pleasing zigzag: the capitals of the piers are cushioned. On the whole, it is much the same as the arch immediately opposite, opening on the south aisle of the nave.

All this side of the transept, with the exception of the small doorway (which was built a few years later), dates from about 1101.

St Catharine's Chapel. — Between the choir aisle entrance and the modern doorway is another Norman arch, which is the entrance to St. Catherine's Chapel — a chantry of Early Decorated style erected on the walls of a former Norman building.

Jefferson says: "In most large churches, altars, distinct from that in the chancel, were founded by wealthy and influential individuals, at which masses might be sung for the repose of the dead; the portion thus set apart, which was generally the east end of one of the aisles, was then denominated a chantry: in it the tomb of the founder was generally placed, and it was separated from the rest of the church by a screen. In the fourteenth century this custom greatly increased, and small additional side aisles and transepts were often annexed to churches and called mortuary chapels; these were used indeed as chantries, but they were more independent in their constitution, and in general more ample in their endowments. The dissolution of all these foundations followed soon after that of the monasteries.

"In the year 1422 Bishop Whelpdale at his death left the 33 sum of £200, for the purpose of founding and endowing a chantry for the performance of religious offices for the souls of Sir Thomas Skelton, knight, and Mr. John Glaston, two gentlemen with whom he had been on terms of intimate friendship, and who were buried in the cathedral. Nicholson thinks it probable this was the chantry of St. Roch; its revenues were valued at £2, 14s. per annum.

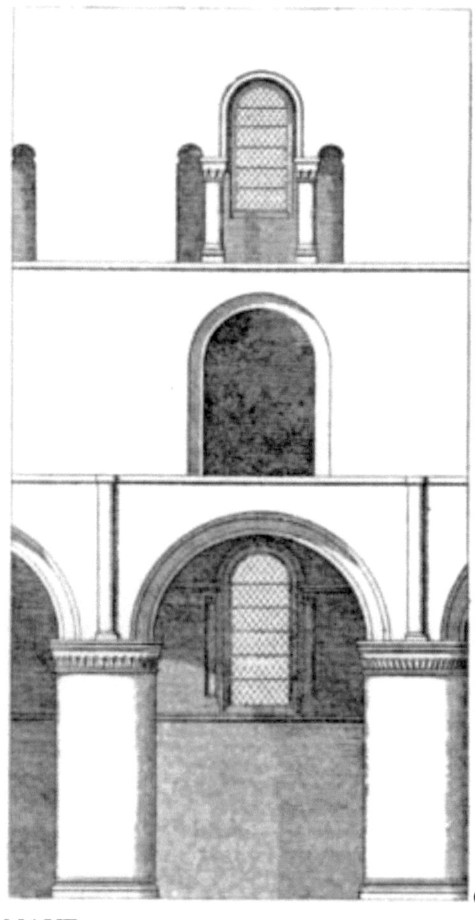ONE BAY OF THE NAVE.

"There was another chantry dedicated to St. Cross; but the period at which, and the person by whom it was founded are not known. It was granted by Edward VI. 'with all messuages, lands, tenements, profits, and hereditaments belonging thereto,' valued at £3, 19s. per annum, to Henry Tanner and Thomas Bucher.

"The chapel of St. Catherine in the Cathedral of Carlisle 34 was founded at an early period by John de Capella, a wealthy citizen, and endowed by him with certain rents, lands, and burgage houses.

In the year 1366 a portion of its revenues being fraudulently detained, Bishop Appleby commanded the chaplains of St. Mary's and St. Cuthbert's to give public notice that the offenders were required to make restitution within ten days on pain of excommunication with bell, book, and candle. Its revenues, according to the rotuli, called the king's books, which were made up in the reign of Henry VIII., were valued at £3, 2s. 8d. per annum."[3]

Some very fine foliated brackets can be seen in the arch between this chapel and the choir aisle.

Dividing the chapel from the transept and aisle is some exquisite carved screen-work (Late Decorated) dating from the latter part of the fifteenth century, and attributed to Prior Gondibour. Its great beauty, and the skilful variations of the designs, will repay careful inspection. The chapel now serves as a vestry for the clergy: but it is to be regretted that it cannot add to the beauty of the cathedral by being utilised for its proper purpose.

The pointed doorway on the left, originally opened on to a well which was closed in the course of the restoration of the building. The position of Carlisle on the border making it liable to sudden attacks in early times, it is probable that the inhabitants may have taken sanctuary in the cathedral many a time, when a well of water would be of great advantage to the refugees.

Monuments in the Transepts.—North Transept. Near the entrance to the north choir aisle stands the altar-tomb of Prior Senhouse. It is covered with a slab of dark blue marble. An inscription runs thus: "The tomb of Simon Senhouse, Prior of Carlisle in the reign of Henry VII. The original inscription being lost, the present plate was substituted by the senior male branch of the Senhouse family, A.D. 1850. Motto, 'Lothe to offend.'"

It was on this tomb that the tenants of the priory were accustomed to pay their rents.35

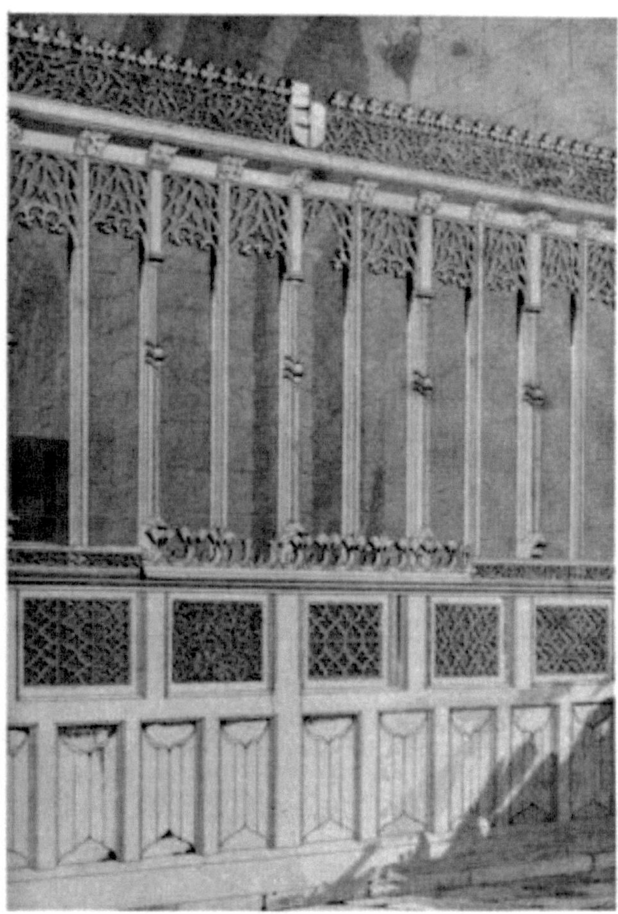

SCREEN—ST. CATHERINE;S CHAPEL.

36South Transept.—On a stone in the west wall (now covered with a pane of glass) is an inscription which was discovered in 1853. It is written in Norse runes, and is as follows:—

"Tolfihn yraita thasi rynr a thisi stain."
"Tolfihn wrote these runes on this stone."

The runes are Norse, not Anglo-Saxon. The latter are not often found, but the former are scarcer still. The runes, perhaps, date from the eleventh century.

There is also a marble tablet containing a medallion likeness of George Moore.

"A man of rare strength and simplicity of character,
of active benevolence and wide influence.
A yeoman's son
he was not born to wealth
but by ability and industry he gained it,
and he ever used it
as a steward of God and a disciple of the Lord Jesus Christ
for the furtherance of all good works."

George Moore was born at Mealsgate, Cumberland, the 9th April 1806. He went to London in 1825. Two years later he was working for Fisher, Stroud & Robinson, lace merchants, as town traveller, and, soon after, as traveller in the north of England. He was so successful that he was nicknamed "The Napoleon of Watling Street." When he was twenty-three he accepted an offer from a firm of lace merchants, Groucock & Copestake, to become a partner. He gave up travelling for orders in 1841, but soon suffered in health. As a remedy he took to following the hounds, and later (in 1844) went on a three months' trip to America. On his return he started on his career of philanthropy which has made him famous. A few of the institutions for which he worked, and to which he contributed largely, may be mentioned; the Cumberland Benevolent Society, the Commercial Travellers' Schools, the British Home for Incurables, the Warehousemen and Clerks' Schools, the Royal Free Hospital, and the London City Mission. Various Cumberland charities found in him a generous supporter. He met with his death in Carlisle. Knocked down by a runaway horse, 20th November 1876, while on his way to attend a meeting of the Nurses' Institution, he died the next day from his injuries. The following was a favourite motto with him: —

"What I spent, I had,
What I saved, I lost,
What I gave, I have."

37

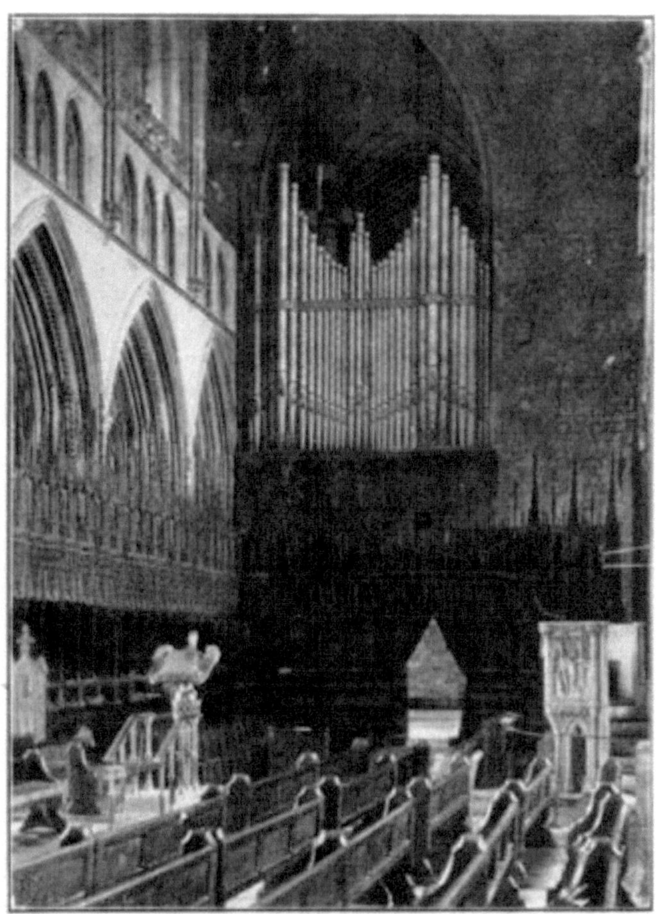

THE CHOIR, LOOKING WEST.

39There is a memorial tablet to Robert Anderson, "the Cumberland Bard," 1770-1833. Born in Carlisle, he had but little schooling,
and at ten years of age he was earning wages as assistant to a calico
printer; later, he was bound apprentice to a pattern-drawer in his
native city. He went to London to pursue his calling, and he seems
to have been led to attempt to write poetry through hearing some
imitation Scottish songs sung at Vauxhall. He published his first
volume in 1798, and his Cumberland Ballads in 1805. His verses, not

altogether destitute of real poetry, are valuable for the pictures they give of obsolete manners and customs of the district.

The **Choir.** — A low doorway in the eastern arch of the tower gives entrance to the choir. Some of the woodwork of the stalls fills the lower part of this arch, and the entrance has been placed towards the north, so as to open exactly on the centre of the choir. In point of beauty the choir compares favourably with any we possess in England, and the eye can rest upon it again and again with renewed satisfaction and delight. Its superb main arcade, with the boldly-designed and finely-carved capitals representing the twelve months of the year — unrivalled in this country; its handsome clerestory windows; its great east window (the pride of the cathedral); and, overhead, its richly-coloured roof, unique in shape, afford a combination not easily to be surpassed.

The choir is about 134 feet long, 34 feet 6 inches wide between the columns, and 72 feet 6 inches between the aisle walls.

The nave is not so wide by about 12 feet, and as the columns of both nave and choir on the south side are on the same line, the extra width is all on the north.

Looking westward, the view is marred by the tower arch not being in the centre of the west wall, in consequence of which there is an ugly space of blank wall between the arch and the north choir aisle.

There are eight bays, averaging about 18 feet in width. 40 Those at the end, however, east and west, are not so wide. At the east they probably suffer from the intrusion of the east wall, which is about six feet thick. The western bays may have lost the space taken for the choir entrance. They have very acute arches, and at the west end rest on responds or half-piers against the tower walls. Those at the east end rest on brackets, and their mouldings lose themselves in the wall on each side of the great window.

The presbytery is reached by two steps from the choir, and the last bay but one (in which the altar stands) is raised three steps above the presbytery.

The main arcade practically dates from after the terrible fire in 1292. The arches escaped, and are splendid specimens of Early English, "of the Pointed style in all the purity of its first period." They were underbuilt with Early Decorated piers, while the capitals were finished at the same time as the triforium and clerestory (Late Decorated) 1350-1400.

The piers are not equal in diameter to those of the nave; they measure but five feet and a quarter. Each consists of eight clustered pillars of red sandstone. The four facing the cardinal points of the compass are larger than the intermediate ones, which are filleted. The base moulding is very deep and hollow. These piers support the Early English arches, with dog-tooth ornament large in the interior, small in the exterior. Altogether, these fine arches give a very pleasing impression of lightness and grace, and make us feel "the fascination of the Pointed style."

At the junctions of the arches are small grotesque heads very well executed. On the north side, where the presbytery begins, is a queen's head, and on the opposite side a figure with a dog's head.

There are altogether fourteen complete, and two half piers, the capitals of which are carved with foliage alone, or with the addition of winged monsters, birds, beasts, and human figures. Twelve of them represent the domestic and agricultural occupations of the months. The first capital on the south side (east end) shows a creature with a man's head, wings, and a tail terminating in the head of a serpent, which bites the monster on the temple. January is symbolised on the next one, and the series continues westward, then crosses over, and proceeds from west to east on the north side, finishing at the last pier but one.

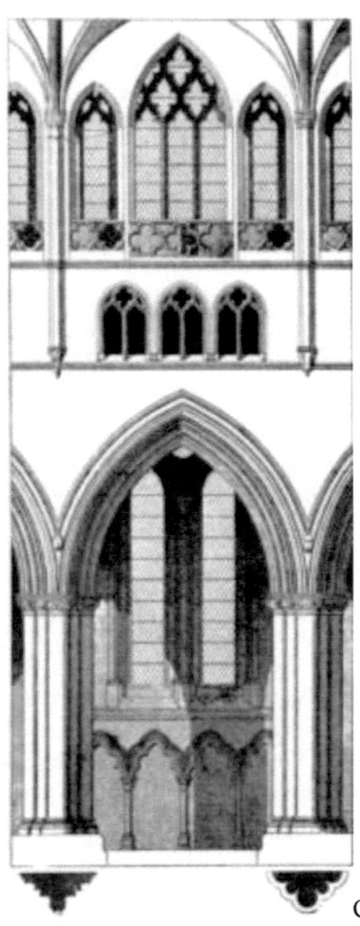

ONE BAY OF THE CHOIR.

41 *January.*—A figure in a loose-fitting tunic, sitting down. He has three faces—two in profile—and is drinking with the right and left mouths. At his feet is a third vessel.

February.—A man in a loose tunic, and head closely wrapped up. He appears to suffer from cold, for his face is woe-begone, and he is sitting over a fire, holding out one boot upside down as if to drain water from it, while he lifts up one foot to catch the heat. The fireplace is very skilfully carved.

March.—A man, hood on head, digging with a spade at the foot of a leafless tree. Other decorations are, a squirrel, a bear with hands, birds, and a beast's body with a mitred head.

April.—A bare-legged man with his head tied up, pruning a tree. On this capital are also two figures half-human, half-bestial, clasping each other round the neck.

May.—A woman in a long gown holding in each hand a bunch of foliage, which she offers to a young 42 man clad in a tunic, with his hood thrown back. In addition there are three winged beasts with human heads, one mitred.

June.—A horseman, bareheaded, holding on his right hand a hawk, and bearing a branch of roses in his left hand. There are also some half-human figures, and men playing musical instruments. This capital is more elaborately carved than any of the others.

July.—A man mowing. In addition there are owls carrying mice in their mouths.

August.—A man working in a wheat-field. He wears a conical hat, and grasps a crutch with one hand while he holds a pruning hook in the other.

September.—A man reaping with a sickle.

October.—A man whose head is tied with a handkerchief; he is engaged in cutting grapes. A fox carrying off a goose is also vigorously carved on this capital.

November.—A man sowing grain from a basket. There is a stag on his right and a horse on his left hand.

December.—A man wearing a loose tunic, who is about to fell an ox which another man holds by the horns. In addition there is a man tending swine.

The last capital shows several heads, and a man sitting on a tree stump.

In each bay of the **Triforium** there are three arches with curvilinear tracery. The principal mullions have octagonal bases. On account of their reduced width, the extreme eastern and western bays have only two arches.

The courses of stone above the base of the triforium are not by any means so smooth and well-proportioned as those beneath. The workmen do not seem to have been actuated by the spirit of those builders "in the elder days of Art" who

> "... wrought with greatest care Each minute and unseen part,
> For the gods see everywhere."

43

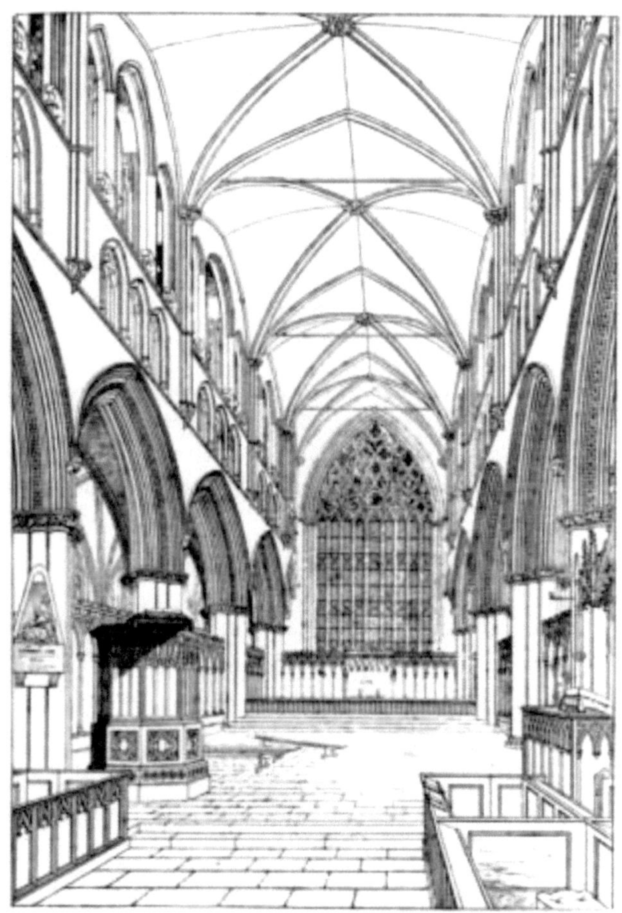

THE CHOIR, LOOKING EAST, IN 1840.

44The **Clerestory** consists of two planes. Each compartment on the face of the choir wall has three high-pitched arches, the middle one being higher than those at the side, and more than twice as wide in the opening. The eastern bay has only the central arch, while the western bay is blank.

The base is decorated with a low parapet pierced with quatrefoils, four in the centre, and two in each side opening. On the south, however, the quatrefoil decoration is slightly different. There are only three quatrefoils in the centre and two smaller ones on each side. This parapet is in great part a restoration, the original having been almost entirely removed, in the vain hope of admitting more light to the lower part of the choir.

In the other plane the windows are in triplets, three lights in the central and single lights on either side, decorated with flamboyant tracery.

The eastern bay has no side lights.

Although the windows seem to be all different, there are but six varieties, distributed as follows:

On the north side beginning at the east the design of the first window is not repeated. That of the next window occurs in the second window on the south side. The third and fifth are alike. The sixth and the last are like the fourth. The design of the seventh window does not occur again.

On the south side one new pattern appears in three windows—the first, fourth, and sixth from the east. The second is like the window opposite, and the third, fifth, and seventh are like the third on the north side.

Of all the windows the second from the east is the most beautiful.

Before 1764 they were filled with stained glass of which some remains are still to be seen. The trefoil heads above the mullions have a brown border with the insertion in some cases of a yellow diamond ornament, and in others of a crown.

The **Roof**—This unique specimen of a waggon-headed ceiling, semi-circular in all its parts, is of oak. Bishop Welton began its construction about 1350. A plaster ceiling, put up in the year 1764, hid this fine timber roof until its removal 45 in 1856. It was then found that enough remained of the original to allow a faithful restoration to be made. But the scheme of colouring—red and green upon white—was not copied. In its stead Owen Jones suggested another—a background of blue plentifully ornamented with golden stars.

The *Saturday Review* is responsible for the statement—for the truth of which, however, it does not vouch—"that on the first occasion when Dean Close found himself beneath the roof, then glowing in all the brilliancy of modern painting and gilding, in semblance of 'the spangled firmament on high,' he solemnly ejaculated, 'Oh my stars!'"

At the triforium base foliated brackets support vaulting shafts of three clustered columns. At the point of contact with the base of the quatrefoil parapet they are ornamented with rings, and their capitals are foliated, but not so naturally as the capitals below. Great semi-circular rafters spring from the capitals and cross the choir. Smaller rafters start from the cornice of the clerestory. These are intersected in the centre of the ceiling by a longitudinal beam. Small moulded ribs divide the space between each great rafter and the longitudinal beam into sixteen panels. The intersections are decorated with carved bosses.

Hammer-beams.—From the foot of three of the principal ribs hammer-beams project. They seem to indicate an intention on the part of the builders to cover the choir with an open-timber roof like that of the Great Hall at Westminster. But having decided on the waggon-headed roof, they did not trouble to remove these beams. Wall pieces and curved struts now connect them with the vaulting shafts, and they have been decorated with "carvèd angels ever eager-eyed, with hair blown back and wings put cross-wise on their breasts."

More than one hundred carved figures ornament the cornice, and the following texts in black-letter appear above them:—

North Side.—Keep thy foot when thou goest to the house of the Lord. (Eccles. v. 1.)

Lift up your hands in the sanctuary and bless the Lord. (Ps. cxxxiv. 2.)

Praise ye the name of the Lord. (Ps. cxxxv. 1.)

Praise God in His sanctuary, (Ps. cl. 1.)

46 Exalt ye the Lord our God and worship at His footstool. (Ps. xcix. 5.)

South Side.—How amiable are Thy tabernacles, O Lord of Hosts! (Ps. lxxxiv. 1.)

My praise shall be of Thee in the great congregation. (Ps. xxii. 25.)

O magnify the Lord with me and let us exalt His name together. (Ps. xxxiv. 3.)

Holiness becometh Thine house for ever. (Ps. xciii. 5.)

The great **East Window** is the crowning ornament and special glory of the cathedral. It is unsurpassed by any other in the kingdom; perhaps there is not a window equal to it in the whole world.

Rickman says: "It is one of the finest if not *the* finest Decorated window in the kingdom. Its elegance of composition and the easy flow of its lines rank it even higher than the celebrated west window of York, which it also excels in the number of divisions. The window is by far the most free and brilliant example of Decorated tracery in the kingdom."

Fergusson, in his "History of Architecture," also praises it: "Its upper part exhibits the most beautiful and perfect design for window tracery in the world. All the parts are in such just harmony the one to the other—the whole is so constructively appropriate and at the same time so artistically elegant—that it stands quite alone, even among windows of its own age."

"The stone-work of all this part (the east window) is entirely new, although it reproduces most minutely the original design" (King, 202-3).

"The whole of the *mouldings,* both of the mullions and tracery, *externally* are nearly destroyed, owing to the perishable nature of the stone with which it is constructed" (Billing, p. 60 (1840)).

This great window almost entirely fills the east end of the choir, being 51 feet high from the sill to the top of the tracery and about 26 feet wide in the clear.

Immediately after the fire in 1292, the work was started, and the jambs with their slender shafts and foliated capitals were erected. Nothing more was done till about the middle of the fourteenth century, when the arch mullions were added; and 47 the tracery dates from about the end of the same century. The mouldings were left unfinished until the restoration of the cathedral, 1856. The tracery (Decorated) is composed of eighty-six pieces struck from 263 centres. Some of the pieces forming the chief divisions are nearly five feet in length. Although the stone-work is modern, the design has been most faithfully copied from the original. In the lower part there are nine lights, no other Decorated window in existence having so many. The west window of Durham Cathedral (partly copied from, but inferior to, the west window of York) and the Rose window in the south transept at Lincoln are of the same character; but that of York ranks next in importance, and is the only window able to compete with the east window of Carlisle.

The design consists of two complete compositions united under one head by interposing a third. The York window, on the contrary, is altogether one complete design, from which no part can be separated without breaking the integrity of the composition.

The width of the opening is the same in both windows, but while the actual tracery of the York window is more than two feet higher, the Carlisle window is greatly superior in the beautiful arch mouldings above its tracery, and also in the side shafts and mouldings.

Again some stiffness is imparted to the design of the York window by the central mullion which reaches from the basement to the top of the arch. The tracery branches outwards from this on each side, and depends upon the arch for support; while the tracery in the Carlisle window is not so dependent. Neither in skilful workmanship nor in variety of ornament is the York window equal to that at Carlisle. With the exception of four quatrefoils (placed above each alternate mullion) it is composed of trefoils. Carlisle, on the contrary, possesses nine quatrefoils, in addition to four placed like those at York. Nearly all the small spandrels formed by the various ornaments are perforated, and this imparts a remarkable air of lightness to the window.

The beautiful stained glass in the tracery is all that remains of the ancient glass. It is of the time of Richard II., and was no doubt preserved because of the expense that reglazing its small intricate forms would have involved.

48 The subject is a Doom—the Resurrection, the Last Judgment, and the New Jerusalem.

"We have our Lord sitting in judgment; the Procession of the Blessed to the Palace of Heaven; the Place of punishment for the wicked; and the general Resurrection.

"The figure of our Saviour is in the uppermost quatrefoil of the central compartment; His countenance will bear the closest inspection; it exhibits evident traces of suffering, but is calm, severe, and dignified. His head is surrounded by a cruciform nimbus. Below this are two quatrefoils, easily distinguished by their silvery appearance. These represent the Procession of the Redeemed to the heavenly Jerusalem, whose towers and pavilions are shown in the quatrefoil to the right. St. Peter stands in the gateway in an attitude of welcome; at his feet flows the River of Life, which some of the Redeemed have reached. The red glare of the Place of punishment makes it easy to be distinguished; the tortures represented are of the most realistic character, and the devils are very material beings, with tails, hoofs, and horns.

"The rest of the picture is occupied with the representation of the general Resurrection:—the dead rising from their graves—ecclesiastics are vested, but laity rise naked, though kings wear their crowns: several bishops are among the crowd, and a pope wearing the triple tiara. Some of the ecclesiastics are bearded, and probably are intended for canons of the cathedral, who, being Austin or Black canons, would wear their beards.

"In one of the quatrefoils, just above the mullions, is a figure surrounded by a heraldic border; this represents John of Gaunt, who was Governor of Carlisle from 1380 to 1384. It is said that he supported the prior, William de Dalston, who refused obedience to the bishop, and had been excommunicated; and that, out of gratitude, he was thus represented in the east window."[4]49

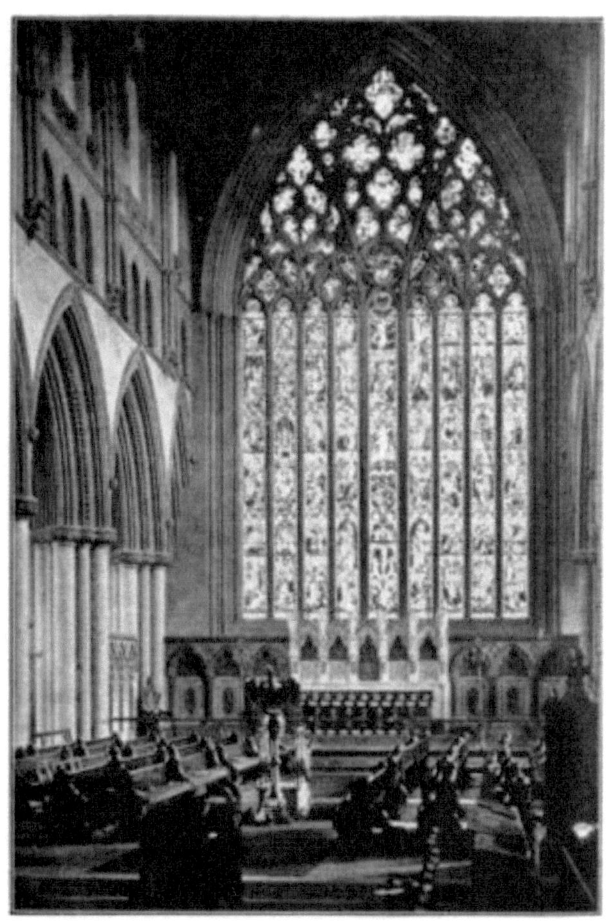

THE CHOIR AND EAST WINDOW.

A "Jesse," which originally filled the lower part of the window, was destroyed at the Reformation. The present glass was inserted in 1861, in memory of Bishop Percy (d. 1856). It represents events in the history of our Lord. Although the colours do not harmonise well with the old glass, they are in accord with the gorgeous colouring of the ceiling. Like most of the stained glass in the cathedral, this is by Hardman of Birmingham. 50

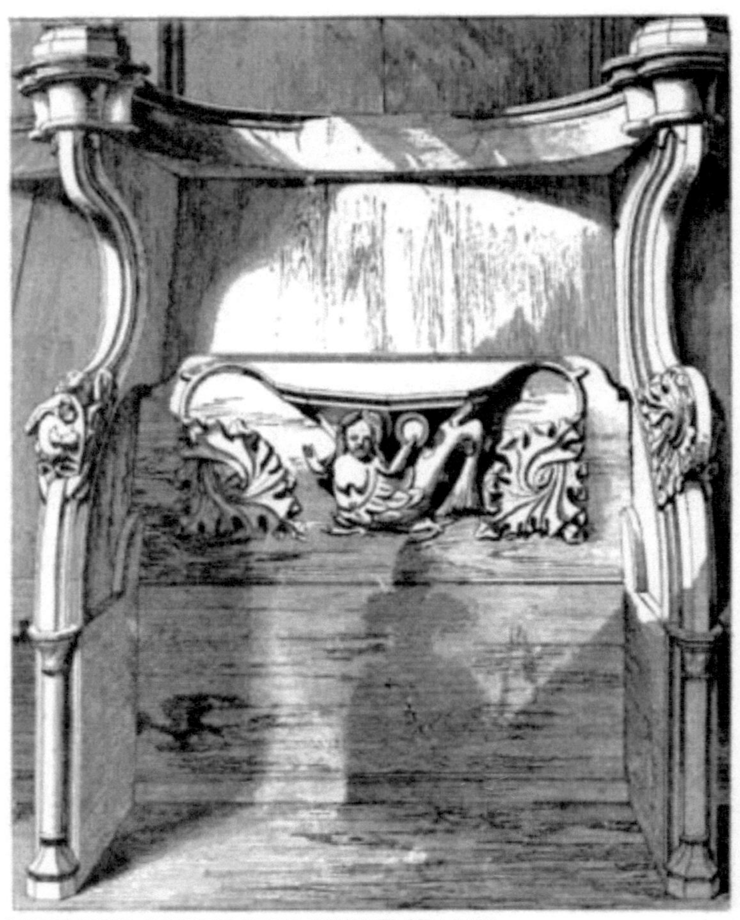

MISERERE, SOUTH SIDE OF THE STALLS.

Bishop Strickland (1399-1413) erected the **Stalls**, which are of black oak, and occupy the three western bays of the choir.

51 Our English cathedrals are far ahead of foreign cathedrals in the beauty and richness of the tabernacle work of their stalls, which in many instances are "like a whole wood, say a thicket of old hawthorn, with its topmost branches spared, slowly transformed into stalls." These in Carlisle, if not among the finest specimens in England, certainly take very high rank.

There are forty-six compartments, divided by fifty columns, upon which the tabernacle work rests. Each compartment consists of a large canopy decorated with quatrefoils, and battlemented. This is surmounted by three smaller canopies and pedestals which were originally occupied by small carved figures. A large pinnacle, richly decorated, like the others, with crockets and finials, finishes the compartment.

Between each stall is a small buttress beginning at the capital and finishing somewhat beneath the top of the large pinnacle. These buttresses have, alternately, a pedestal with a canopy above; and a pedestal supporting a small flying-buttress terminating in a pinnacle enriched with small crockets.

Prior Haithwaite is said to have added the tabernacle-work after the year 1430.

The division between each stall shows either a well-executed foliated ornament, or an angel. In the north-west and south-west angles the elbows of the seats are carved with the head of a king supposed to represent Henry IV. The panels of the desks are elaborately worked, and the stone plinth which supports them is decorated with quatrefoils.

The stalls at the west end of the choir are wider than the others, and are used by the higher dignitaries of the cathedral.

The Dean's stall is on the left of the choir entrance, and the Bishop's on the right. This arrangement is said to have existed since the time of æthelwulf. He was the first prior, and upon his elevation to the bishopric he still kept the prior's seat.

The hinged seats, known as misereres or misericordes, were constructed to keep the monks from falling asleep while at prayers. The carvings beneath these seats are of different designs, generally grotesque.

The following is a list of the subjects found carved thereon:—52

NORTH SIDE	**SOUTH SIDE**
A dragon swallowing a man.	Two angels.
Bird and young.	Dragon.
Dragon and lions.	Bird and beast fighting.

Three dragons, one with a human face.
Winged figure with a tabour.
Dragon devouring a bird.
Coronation of the Virgin.
Three griffins.
Pelican in its act of piety.
Dragon and lion fighting.
Griffin and two young ones.
Two dragons joined together.
Two storks eating out of a sack.
Figure with wings, claws, and human face.
Angelic musician.
Two eagles.
Double-headed eagle.
Fox and goose.
Two dragon bodies with a human head.
Angel playing an instrument.
A man with two eagles plucking his beard.
Dragon, and two lions with human faces.

Human head on two animal bodies.
Winged dragon.
Winged serpent.
Two beasts with one head.
Two men fighting.
Griffin with human head.
Dragon and foliage.
Two eagles holding the head of a beast.
Fox and goose.
Human figure with four wings.
Man and dragon fighting.
Angel bearing a shield.
Angel and dragons.
Pelican in its act of piety.
Boar killing a man.
Man holding two dragons.
Dragon killing a beast.
Mermaid.
Dragon and lion in combat.

The **Salkeld Screen.**—On the north side of the choir, the westernmost bay of the presbytery is filled by a fine wooden screen of Renaissance work, erected about 1542 by Lancelot Salkeld, last prior and first dean of Carlisle. It is divided into three compartments; through the central one entrance could be gained to the choir formerly by an ascent of three steps from the north choir aisle.

It is very elaborate, and some portions are very beautiful. The lower part is panelled, each panel having two heads carved in bas-relief. The upper part is of well-executed tracery work.

Over each compartment is a pediment decorated in the centre with shields. The western one has been restored. The initials L.S. and D.K. (Lancelot Salkeld, Decanus Karliolensis) occur on the screen. The other bays were originally filled with screen-work similar to that in St. Catherine's Chapel. In 1764 these screens were removed and stored in the Fratry crypt as lumber. In the end they were used as firewood; only a few pieces preserved by the neighbouring 53 gentry escaping destruction. A stone screen now surrounds the sacrarium on three sides. The reredos is higher than this screen. It is arcaded, and its compartments have triangular-headed canopies and some well-executed figures. The late Mr. Street designed it, and its cost was £1790.

The **Bishop's Throne**, of English and foreign oak, was also designed by the late Mr. Street. The canopy of the throne is nearly thirty feet high.

The **Pulpit** is a memorial of Archdeacon Paley, who is buried close at hand in the north choir aisle. It is of richly-carved Caen stone, on a plinth of black Manx marble, and ornamented with carvings in white alabaster, of scenes from the New Testament. In shape it is hexagonal, with shafts at the angles rising into an enriched cornice. The lectern—a brass eagle—was given in memory of the late G.C. Mounsey, sometime diocesan registrar.

In the middle of the choir is a monument to Bishop Bell. On a blue slab under a triple canopy, the centre pediment of which has I.H.S., and its point the Deity and Christ, is a brass figure of a bishop *in pontificalibus*, mitre and gloves; his right hand holds on his breast an open book inscribed —

Hec mea
Spes in sinu meo

His left hand, over which hangs the maniple, has a rich crosier. On a semi-circular scroll over his head —

Credo q^d redemptor meus vivit et novissio die de terra surrectur
su et in Carne mea videbo deu salvatore275; meu.

Under his feet —

Hac marmor fossa Bell presulis en tenet ossa
Duresme dudu prior his post pontificatu
Gessit atq' renuit primum super omia querit
Dispiciens mudu poscendo pramia fratru

On the ledge round the slab —

Hic jacet Reverendus Pater Ricardus Bell quondam Episcopus Karleolensis qui ab hac luce migravit videlicet vicesimo Quarto die ... Anno Domini.... Et omnium fidelium defunctorum. per misericordiam dei requiescant in perpetua pace. Amen."

54 The ancient high altar probably stood one bay nearer to the west than the present altar. There, in the presence of Bishop Halton, Robert Bruce took an oath of fidelity to Edward I. Ten years later he proved false to this oath, and the Papal Legate solemnly excommunicated him with bell, book, and candle.

Very shortly after this, Edward I. dedicated the litter in which he had journeyed thus far, and mounting his horse at the cathedral door rode through the priory gateway bent on the conquest of Scotland. He never lived to reach that country, for he died in sight of the Scottish coast at Burgh-on-Sands.

North Choir Aisle.—This aisle is entered by a handsome Decorated arch, a very good example of thirteenth-century work.

The north wall, with the exquisite two-light lancet windows, is Early English, and dates from the period immediately after the demolition of the Norman choir about 1260.

Each compartment of the cinquefoil **wall-arcade** is separated by triple columns, and the space divided into four parts by shafts, barely detached from the wall, supporting foliated arches. This is the general description for both north and south choir aisles.

The eastern bay belongs to the retro-choir, and is of later date.

Above the wall-arcade are the graceful two-light lancet windows, with their slender columns, deep mouldings, and rich dog-tooth decoration.

In each bay there are four divisions; the two outer ones blank, and the two others forming the window. The shafts are detached from the wall; the central one is higher than the rest, and its capital is foliated. From the outer columns in the blank divisions, the shoulder, or hipped rib, after rising a short distance, sinks to the level of the capitals of the vaulting columns. At the side of the window columns two small circular mouldings, decorated with small dog-tooth ornament, continue without a break round the head of each window. A large blank quatrefoil is inserted in the space between the lights and the outer arch moulding.55

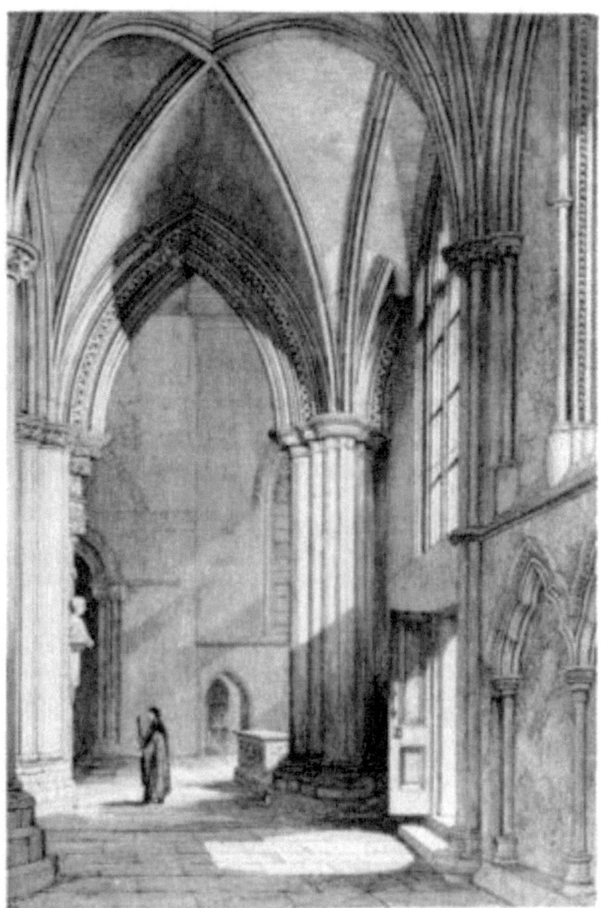

NORTH AISLE OF THE CHOIR.

The corner column (north side of entrance) has been inserted by cutting away part of the east wall of the north transept. 56Like the aisle it dates from about the last half of the thirteenth century. On its capital there is the spring of a pointed arch, enriched with dog-tooth ornament similar to the entrance arch.

Probably it was intended to pull the north transept down, and re-build it with the addition of an eastern aisle. This column would then have been part of it. The existence of an offset on the north face of the aisle wall, with the return of the base-course and string-course upon it, seems to add weight to this theory.

The nearest clustered column to it has also been altered, and consists of five shafts instead of three. A rib springs from the additional shafts to the centre of the corner column. There are also remains of groining like that of the aisle.

The bay near the entrance has a window (Perpendicular) dating from after the Civil Wars. Beneath this there was formerly an entrance to the cathedral. This has now been walled up.

The groined stone roof dates from after 1292, although, perhaps, it is composed of materials of an earlier date.

On the south side of the entrance is a very beautiful foliated bracket; the foliated boss at its base was at one time ornamented with a very fine knot.

Monuments in North Choir Aisles.—In the third bay from the east are two low-arched recesses. Being of the same date as the aisle, they may have been intended to receive the statues of the bishops who did their best to repair the ravages of the fire in 1292. The arches are almost flat, and decorated with a kind of chevron moulding very rarely met with. In Burpham Church, Sussex, there is another example of this moulding applied to the decoration of the south side of the south transept arch.

A bishop's effigy is in the eastern recess. It is of Early English date; and before 1292 was situated within the choir. Afterwards a niche was cut in the fourth bay from the east for its reception. It was eventually placed in its present position at the time of the restoration of the cathedral, and the other niche filled up. It may possibly represent Bishop Silvester of Everdon. It has suffered damage during its migrations in the cathedral; and the feet are broken. This was probably done when it was removed from the choir to the 57 aisle (1856). Jewels which originally enriched the mitre and the cross on the breast have disappeared.

In the next bay to the east is a small mural brass plate finely engraved in memory of Bishop Robinson (1598-1616.) He was a native of Carlisle, and, entering Queen's College, Oxford, as a "poor serving child," eventually became provost, and proved a great benefactor to that foundation.

"The bishop is represented *in pontificalibus*, kneeling, with one hand supporting a crosier; the other is sustaining a lighted candle, and holding a cord to which three dogs are attached, who appear guarding an equal number of sheepfolds from the attack of wolves. Below the candle is a group of figures bearing implements of agriculture and peaceful industry; near their feet is a wolf playing with a lamb; and various warlike instruments scattered and broken. Each part is illustrated with appropriate Greek and Latin sentences chiefly selected from the Scriptures. Behind the bishop is a quadrangular building, enclosing an open court, and apparently intended to represent the college which he had so much benefited.

"Over the gateway is a shield charged with three spread eagles, being the arms of Robert Eglesfield, the founder of that college; on the college are the words, *Invenit destructum; reliquit extructum et instructum* (he found it destroyed; he left it built and furnished). Above this building is the delineation of a cathedral; over the entrance is inscribed — *Intravit per ostium* (he entered by the door); on a label across the entrance is *Permansit fidelis* (he endured faithful to the end), and below, on the steps, under a group of figures, one of whom is kneeling and receiving a benediction, are the words, *Recessit beatus* (he departed blessed). Near the top of the plate is the angel of the Lord bearing a label inscribed in Greek characters, *Tois Episcopois* (Unto the Bishops).

"Above are the words, *Erant pastores in eadem regione excubantes et agentes vigilias noctis super gregem suum* (there were in the same country shepherds abiding in the field and keeping watch over their flocks by night). At the bottom of the plate in the cathedral is a Latin inscription to this effect: 'To Henry Robinson of Carlisle, D.D., a most careful provost of Queen's College, Oxon, and afterwards a most watchful bishop of this church for eighteen years, who on the 13th Calend of July in the year from the delivery of the Virgin, 1616, and of his age 64, devoutly resigned his spirit unto the Lord.

Bernard Robinson, his brother and heir, set up this memorial as a testimony of his love.'"[5]

About halfway up the aisle Archdeacon Paley lies buried between his two wives, Jane (d. 1791), and Catherine (d. 1819). On a brass plate in the centre of the stone is the following inscription:—

Here lie
interred the remains
of
William Paley, D.D.
who died May 25th
1805
Aged 62 years.

Archdeacon Paley wrote both of his well-known works, "Horæ Paulinæ" and "Evidences of Christianity," at Carlisle.

Legendary Paintings.—Between the bays east and west of the Salkeld screen there is a broad stone plinth panelled in front. The stalls stand on the plinth west of the screen, and the backs are painted with scenes from the monkish legends of St. Anthony the Hermit, St. Cuthbert, and, in the south choir aisle, St. Augustine. A rhymed couplet explains each picture; and the paintings, though rudely executed, give good examples of late fifteenth-century dress and ornament. Prior Gondibour caused the work to be done, and as Richard Bell was bishop at the time he may have suggested illustrating the life of St. Cuthbert, who was really the first bishop of Carlisle, and whose body was enshrined at Durham, where Bell had been prior before his elevation to the bishopric.

The following is a detailed account of the *Legendary Paintings,* with short note of the principal persons therein represented:—

St. Cuthbert was born in the Lothians; at eight years he was living under the care of a widow in the village of Wrangholm.

In 651 while keeping watch over his master's flocks near the Lauder, which flows into the Tweed, he had a vision of the soul of Bishop Aidan being carried up to heaven by angels. A few days after, he heard of the death of the good bishop, and straightway journeyed to the monastery of Melrose. Here he was accepted, and in a short time received the tonsure.

59 The Northumbrian peasants at this time were, mostly, only Christians in name. Cuthbert wandered among them, choosing the most out-of-the-way villages, where other teachers would not go. "He needed no interpreter as he passed from village to village; the frugal long-headed Northumbrians listened willingly to one who was himself a peasant of the Lowlands and who had caught the rough Northumbrian burr. His patience, his humorous good sense, the sweetness of his look, told for him, and not less the vigorous frame which fitted the peasant-preacher for the hard life he had chosen.

"Never did man die of hunger who served God faithfully," he would say, when nightfall found them supperless in the waste. "Look at the eagle overhead! God can feed us through him if he will"—and once at least he owed his meal to a fish that the scared bird let fall.

In 664 he was made prior of Lindisfarne. "Gentle with others, he was severe with himself, and was unsparing in his acts of mortification and devotion."

In 676 he retired, first to a cave near Howburn, and later to Fame Island, where he remained in strict seclusion for nine years.

He was elected bishop of Hexham in 684, and with much difficulty was persuaded to undertake the duties. He soon exchanged Hexham for Lindisfarne.

As bishop, Cuthbert was diligent in preaching, protected the poor from their oppressors, lived on very little, and fed and clothed the poor.

Towards the end of 686 he gave up his bishopric and returned to his beloved Fame Island, where he died in March 687.

ST. CUTHBERT

1. Her Cuthbert was forbid layks and plays
   As S. Bede i' hys story says.

2. Her the angel did hym eale
   And made hys grievous sore to hele.

3. Her saw he Aydan's sawl up go
   to hevyn bliss wth angels two.

4. Her to hym and hys palfray
   God send hem fude in hys jornay.

5. Her on Melross for to converse
   With hy Bosle and laws reherse.

6. The angel he did as gest refreshe
   With met and drynk and hys fete weshe

7. Her Basel told hy yt he must de
   60 And after yt bysshop should be

8. Her to hys breder and pepyl eke
   He preched godys word myld and mek

9. Her stude he naked in ye see
   till all David psalms sayd had he.

10. He was gydyd by ye egle fre
    And fed wth ye delfyne as ye see

11. Fresh water god sent owt of ye ston
    to hym in Farn and befor was noon

12. Consecrate byshop yai made hy her
    off Lyndisfarne both far and nere.

13. Her by prayers fendys out Farne glad
    and wth angel hads hys hous made

14. To thys child god grace (here gave) he
    Thro hys prayers as ye may se.

15. Byshop two yerys when he had beyn
    In Farne he died both holy and clene

16. The crowys y^t did his hous unthek
    This for full low fell at hys fete

17. xi yere after yt beryd was he
    Yai fand hym hole as red may ye.

St. Anthony, one of the primitive hermits, and the founder of monasticism, was born at Coma, in Upper Egypt, in A.D. 251. Before he was twenty years old he lost his parents, and inherited great riches from them, but within a year he sold all that he had and gave the money to the poor. He then retired into solitude near Coma, passing his time in manual labour, prayer, and study. Later, he went farther into the wilderness, and lived in a cave. Satan is said to have tempted him by sending spirits to him, disguised as beautiful women. Finding this ineffectual, it is related that the Evil One made a violent attack on him, and beat him so severely that he left him for dead. At the age of ninety he heard of another hermit (St. Paul the Hermit), and made a journey to visit him. St. Paul died soon after this meeting, and St. Anthony, aided by two lions, buried him. In his 105th year he told some of his disciples that he was going to die; then, accompanied by a few monks, he retired deeper into the wilderness, where he died, having first obtained a promise that they would keep the place of his burial secret.

(In the time of Innocent IV. all hermits who lived under no 61 recognised discipline were incorporated and reduced under the rule of St. Augustine.)

THE LEGEND OF ST. ANTHONY

1. Of Anton story who lyste to here
   In Egypt was he bornt as doyth aper.

2. Her is he babtyd, Anton they hym call
   Gret landes and renttes to hym doeth fawl.

3. As scoler to the kyrk here is he gayn
   To here the sermontt and aftyr itt he's tayn.

4. Here geyffith he to the kyrk boith land and rent
   To leve in povert is hys intent.

5. Here in Agello to oon oulde man he wentt
   To lerne perfeccion is hys intent.

6. Here makyth he breder as men of relig',
   And techyth them vertu to leve in perfecco.

7. Here to the wyldernes as armet geon he
   And thus temptyth hym covytice with oon gold dyshie.

8. The sprytt of fornycacon to hy her doth apper
   And thus he chastith his body with thorne and brer.

9. The devill thus hat hy wounded w_t lance and staf
   And levyth hy for deyd lyying at his cayf

10. Here Crist haith hym helyd the devill he doth away
    And comfortyd his confessor deyd as he lay

11. Here comands he y^{is} bests and ffast away th$_a$ flie

     Ye bor hy obbays and wth hy bydeds he.

12. Here makyth he a well and water hath uptayne
    And comforted hys breder thyrst was nere slayn.

13. Here commandith he best to make hy a cayf
    And thus he berys Paulyn and lay hy in graf

14. Thus walkèd he over the flode water doth hy no der
    Theodor hy se and dare nou cu hy nere

15. Here departith Anton, to hevyn his saul is gone
    Betwixt his two breder in wilder's the alone.

16. Here in wilderns they bery hym that no man shud him knaw
    For soo he comanded syne hom first tha draw.

17. Thus levyth he i wildern's xxⁱⁱ yere and more
    Without any company bot the wylde boore.

St. Augustine, the first great saint of the Order, and patron of the canons of the cathedral. He was born at Tagaste, in Numidia, A.D. 354. His father, Patricius, was a Pagan, while his mother, Monica, was a Christian. Patricius, perceiving the 62 ability of his son, "spared nothing to breed him up a scholar." When quite young he had a severe illness, and expressed a wish to be baptized, but on his recovery the wish vanished. Later, his morals grew corrupt, and he lived a profligate life until he became a convert of the Manicheans at the age of nineteen. After teaching grammar at Tagaste, and rhetoric at Carthage, he proceeded to Rome, against the wish of Monica. He next became professor of rhetoric at Milan. Ambrose was then archbishop, and through listening to his preaching, St. Augustine abandoned the Manichean doctrines, and was baptized at Easter the following year, A.D. 387. Monica, who had prayed unceasingly for his conversion, now visited him at Milan, and was greatly rejoiced at the answer to her prayers. His mother started to return to Africa with her son, but died at Ostia. At a villa outside Hippo, St. Augustine passed three years in the company of eleven pious men. "They had all things in common as in the early Church; and fasting and prayer, Scripture-reading and almsgiving, formed their regular occupations. Their mode of life was not formally monastic according to any special rule, but the experience of this time of seclusion was, no doubt, the basis of that monastic system which St. Augus-

tine afterwards sketched, and which derived from him its name."
He then entered the priesthood, A.D. 390, and five years afterward
was made coadjutor in the bishopric of Hippo, and eventually became bishop. The rest of his life he devoted to defending the Christian religion, both by preaching and by writing. He died in Hippo,
A.D. 430, while the Vandals were besieging it. St. Augustine is
called "the greatest of the Fathers." His great work "De Civitate Dei,"
"the highest expression of his thought," engaged him for seventeen
years. In his well-known "Confessions" is given an account of his
spiritual progress, and of his state before he was converted.63

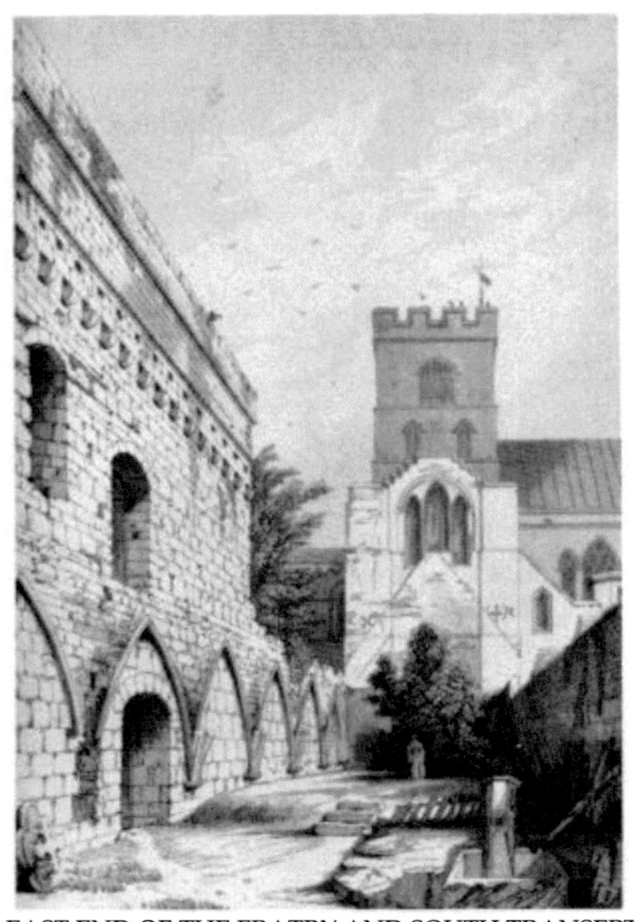

EAST END OF THE FRATRY AND SOUTH TRANSEPT.

64

ST. AUGUSTINE

1. Her fader and mod[r] of sanct Austyne
   Fyrst put hym her to lerne doctryne

2. Her taught he gramor and rethorike
   Emongys all doctors non was hy lyke

3. Her promysed he wth hys moder to abide

Bot he left her wepyng and stal yᵉ tyde grace de diu
   (on the ship's sail)

4. There taught he at rome the sevyn science
   Yᵗ was gret prece tyll hys presence

5. Her prechyd Ambrose and oft tymys previd
   Qd lettera occidₜ wych Austin mevid

6. Her Poinciane hym tald ye lyffe of Sanct Anton
   And to Elipius he stonyshed said thus anone
   Qᵈ patimʳ surguᵗ indocti et Cœluᵐ rapiu't
   Et nos cu doctrinis i inferᵣ demergimur

7. Her sore wepying for hys gret syn
   He went to morne a garth wythin

8. Her wepyng and walyng as he lay
   Sodenly a voice thus herd he say
   Tolle lege Tolle lege

9. No word for tothewarke here myght he say
   But wrote to the pepil for him to pray

10. Her of Sainct Ambrose chrysteyned was

11. The gret doctor Austyne throgh Godes grace
   Te Deum laudamus Te Domᵐ confitemur

12. Her deyd his moder called Monica
   As thai were returning in to Affrica

13. Her was he sacred prest and usyd
   Of Valery the Bishop thoffe he refusyt

14. Her after (Godes word mylde and mek taught he)
   Hys (men of) religion as ye may see

15. Her fortunate the heretyk concludit he
   Informyng the laws of Maneche

16. Consecrate Byshop was this doctour
   By all the cuntre with gret honour

17. As yₛ woman come to hy for consolacion
   She saw hym wth the Trinite in meditacion

18. When he Complyn had said and come to luke
   He was full cleyn owt of yˢ knafys buke
   (Penitet me tibi ostendisse librum)

19. They beried hys body wyth deligence
    her in hys aun kirk of Yponese.

20. Her Lied-brand the kyng of Luberdy
    Hym translate frō Sardyne to Pavye

21. Thei shrynyd hys banes solemnly
    In sanct Peter kyrk thus at Pavye

22. Thys prior he bad soon do evynsang her
    And helyd hym that was sek thre yer

23. Her he apperyd unto these men thre
    And bad yam go to . . . . . . yᵗ hale

65

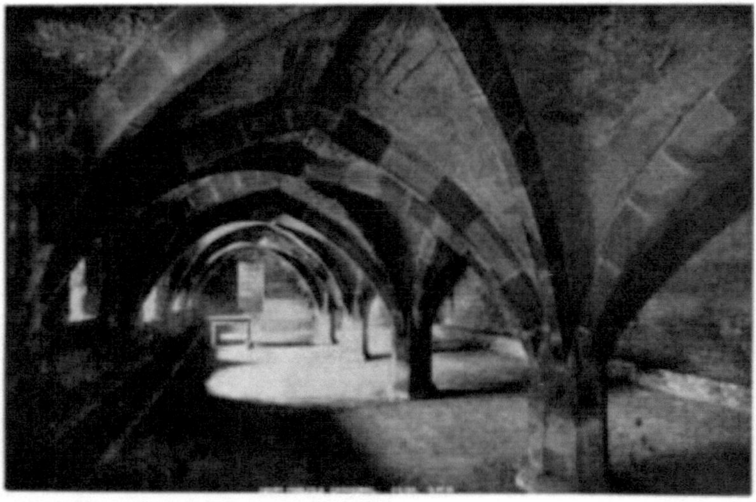

THE CRYPT UNDER THE FRATRY.

66 Between the compartments devoted to the lives and deeds of
St. Anthony and St. Cuthbert are pictures of the twelve Apostles
with the words which, according to tradition, each one contributed
to the Creed.

APOSTLES AND CREED

ST. PETER   I believe in God the Father Almighty, Maker
of heaven and earth

ST. ANDREW	And in Jesus Christ His only Son our Lord
ST. JAMES	Who was conceived by the Holy Ghost, born of the Virgin Mary
ST. JOHN	He suffered under Pontius Pilate, was crucified, dead, and buried
ST. THOMAS	He descended into Hell: rose again the third day from the dead
ST. JAMES	And sitteth on the right hand of God the Father Almighty
ST. PHILIP	From whence He shall come to judge the quick and the dead.
ST. BARTHOLO-MEW	I believe in the Holy Ghost
ST. MATTHEW	The Communion of Saints
ST. SIMON	The Forgiveness of Sins
ST. THADDEUS	The Resurrection of the Body
ST. MATTHIAS	And the Life Everlasting.

At the time of the Reformation these paintings were all white-washed. Dean Percy (1778) removed the whitewash from some of them, and they are now all restored to their original condition as far as possible.

Retro-choir. — The extreme eastern bay of each aisle, and the passage behind the altar, form the retro-choir, which is Late Decorated.

Its acutely-pointed windows are practically of identical pattern, the mullions and side-mouldings having richly floriated capitals.

The last arch of the main arcade is supported by a bracket of foliage. A fragment of rib still remaining was for the cross-groining of the aisle; but as this would have interfered with the arch mouldings, the rib was terminated higher up the wall upon a bracket in the form of a crouching figure.

The wall-arcade has three divisions, the capitals of the columns are foliated, and the point where the hood mouldings meet is ornamented with the carving of a human head.

The low doorway forms the entrance to a staircase leading to the upper part of the cathedral, and the belfry.

67 Beneath the great east window there is a plain tablet in memory of Archdeacon Paley, and another in memory of his two wives and infant son.

Another tablet is in memory of Dean Cramer: "Apud Oxonienses Historiæ Profr. Regius," died 1848.

Opposite is a monument to Bishop Law, the work of T. Banks, R.A. A figure of Religion leaning on a cross is above the tablet. This monument was originally fixed on the pillar behind the pulpit ("Columnæ hujus sepultus est ad pedem"). It was removed to the north aisle because of the weakening of the pillar through having been cut to receive the memorial; and in 1894 was again removed and fixed here, about as far away from the bishop's grave as it could possibly be placed.

Under the great window, a little to the south, is a tombstone, similar to that of Bishop Bell in the choir, but the brass is missing.

On the south side the last arch of the main arcade is supported by a bracket representing a human figure sustaining mouldings, resembling the one at the end of the north aisle.

The small east window is in memory of John Heysham, M.D. (1753-1834). He graduated at Edinburgh in 1777, and settled in Carlisle where he practised till his death. He is famous for his statistical observations; a record of the annual births, marriages, diseases, and deaths in Carlisle (ten years to 1788); a census of the inhabitants in 1780 and 1788. The actuary of the Sun Life Assurance Office used these statistics as the basis of the well-known "Carlisle Table of Mortality." Aided by the dean and chapter he established the first dispensary for the poor at Carlisle. He died in 1834, and was buried in St. Mary's Church.

One of the heads ornamenting the wall-arcade is said to represent Edward I.

The **South Choir Aisle** is in most particulars the same as the corresponding aisle on the north. The windows of its two bays next to St. Catherine's Chapel are Early English of a later period than the others, but the effect they produce is not by any means so pleasing. The decorations of the capitals of the Early English columns are not so elaborate as those in the north choir aisle.

In the third bay east of St. Catherine's Chapel, two arches of the wall-arcade have been thrown into one, forming a 68 doorway. The arch is formed by seven segments, and its hood-moulding terminates in the cornice immediately above the arcade.

Monuments in South Choir Aisle.—At the east end is an altar tomb with recumbent effigy in white marble, of Bishop Waldegrave, by H.H. Armstead, R.A.

The words "væ mihi si non evangelizavero" (i Cor. ix. 16) are on the edge of the upper part of the tomb. Below this is the following inscription:—

Samuel Waldegrave
57th Bishop of Carlisle
Born Sept. 13, 1817; Consecrated, Nov. 12, 1860;
Entered into rest Oct. 1, 1869.
"To me to live is Christ and to die is gain."

Phil. i. 21.

A tribute of
Affection, Admiration, and Respect.
Raised by public subscription.

A.D. 1872.

A recess with low pointed arch beneath the third window from the east formerly contained a monument to Sir John Skelton, Knt. (1413-22).

Outside St. Catherine's Chapel is an altar tomb with a damaged effigy in red sandstone of Bishop Barrow (1423-29). Originally it was painted and gilt, and, although greatly injured, the remains show that the statue was well executed.

Opposite, under a carved oak canopy, is a bronze recumbent figure by Hamo Thornycroft, R.A., of Harvey Goodwin. The following is inscribed on a bronze tablet:

In memory of Harvey Goodwin,
Fifty-eighth Bishop of Carlisle.
at Cambridge, and Ely, and in this diocese
a proved leader of men.
Learned, eloquent, wise, untiring,
he used his rare gifts of mind and heart
in the service of his master
for the good of the English people,
and of the Church of Christ at home and abroad.
Born, Oct. 9, 1818; Consecrated, Nov. 30, 1869; Died, Nov. 25, 1891.

Next to this, under a richly-carved canopy, is a recumbent figure in white marble, by H.H. Armstead, R.A., of Dean Close. The monument bears the following inscription: — 69

Francis Close, D.D.,
25 years Dean of this cathedral, died 1882, aged 85.
Erected by public subscription as a mark
of affection and esteem (1884).

The canopy, given by his son, bears the words following: "This canopy was erected by Admiral Close in memory of his father."

Francis Close was born in 1797, and was educated at St. John's, Cambridge. From 1826 till 1856 he held the living of Cheltenham. He was a liberal subscriber to societies for various philanthropic purposes whether in connection with the Established Church or not. In 1856 he was nominated Dean of Carlisle. Although a very popular preacher his theological views were far from broad. He was, also, a strenuous opponent of betting, theatre-going, indulgence in alcoholic liquors, and smoking. The poor people of Carlisle lost a good friend when he passed away. His failing health obliged him to give up the deanery in 1881, and at the end of the following year he died at Penzance, where he was wintering.

The fourth window is filled with glass in memory of members of the Mounsey family, and Captain John Oswald Lambert.

The following subjects are represented: —

Our Lord rebuking the Sea.	The Transfiguration.	Pilate writing the title for the Cross.
The Adoration of the Magi.	The entry into Jerusalem.	Our Lord before Pilate.
St. Paul before the Chief Priests.	St. Paul before King Agrippa.	St. Paul on board ship.

At the back of the bishop's throne are some shelves containing a few standard devotional books for the use of the congregation before and after divine service. It would be a good thing if this custom could be generally adopted, and every church in the land furnished with a small library of the works of such men as Thomas a Kempis, St. Augustine, Taylor, Law, and Keble.

The low doorway in the north-eastern angle of the retro-choir opens on a staircase leading to the upper part of the cathedral, and the tower.

70 If we ascend to the clerestory we may pass along the ambulatory, and obtain a nearer view of the great east window (especially the old glass in the tracery), the choir roof, and the clerestory windows. At the end of the ambulatory we come to the belfry.

There are six **Bells**, one of which, bearing the date 1396, was furnished by Bishop Strickland. It is inscribed as follows: —

In: voce: sum: munda: maria;
sonando: secunda.

Another bell bears the following sentence: —

"Jesus be our speed." Date 1608.

A third has on the rim—"This ringe was made six tuneable bells at the charge of the Lord Howard and other gentree of the country and citie, and officers of the garrisson, by the advice of Majer Jeremiah Tolhurst, governor of the garrisson 1658." This bell was cracked while ringing during the rejoicings held in honour of the peace after Waterloo.

On a bell dated 1657 can be read, "I warne you how your time doth pass away, Serve God therefore while life doth last, and say Glorie in excelsis Deo."

Of the remaining bells, one is dated 1659, and the other 1728.

In war time the tower was useful as a watch-tower, especially when the enemy was approaching from Scotland. The small turret was used for fire signals.

There is an interesting record in connection with the tower which is found in an account of the trial of the Governor of Carlisle in 1745. It is as follows: —

"I desired that two men might be posted upon the high Tower of the Cathedral with a very large spying glass I had brought with me, and to send me a report of what they observed in the country. The Chancellor proposed to the clergy to take this duty, which they readily did, and were very exact and vigilant, and when the Rebells came before Carlisle they took up arms as Volunteers most of whom served under me as aides-de-camp."[6]71

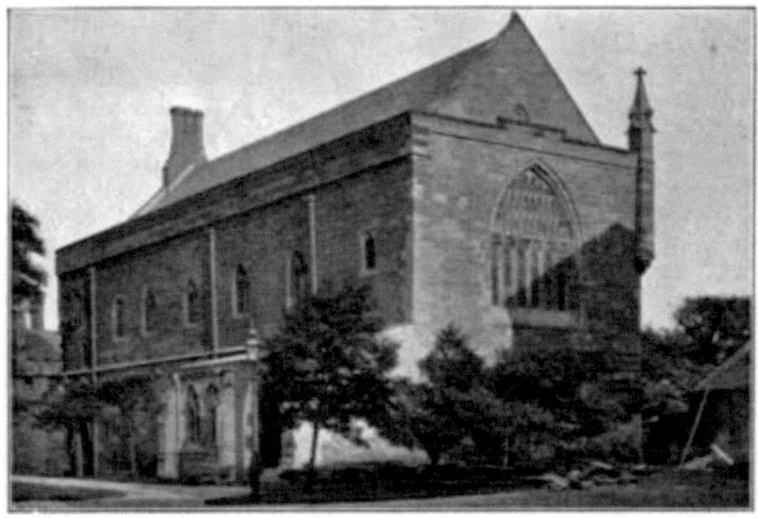

THE FRATRY.

The Monastic Buildings

73The Monastic Buildings were erected on the land south of the cathedral. The cloisters, enclosing a large open court, stood west of the south transept, communicating with the two doors — one in the north-east angle, the other in the north-west.

The dormitory, built upon an arcade, was joined to the south transept, and had a door opening into it above the present modern doorway.

West of the dormitory, and parallel with the nave, was the fratry; adjoining the east end of which, and stretching to the south-east, were the domestic offices.

West of the fratry was the prior's lodging (now the deanery).

The chapter-house, which was built somewhere in the angle formed by the choir and the dormitory, has disappeared entirely. It was octagonal in shape, about 28 feet across, and had a conical roof.

The great fire in 1292 caused great destruction to the priory buildings. They were put up again about 1350, and Prior Gondibur almost entirely rebuilt them towards the end of the fifteenth century.

There is no reason for doubting that the various buildings were handed over in good order at the dissolution of the priory. The destruction which has left standing only the fratry, the prior's lodging, and the gate tower (1528), was the act of the Parliamentary troops and their Scottish allies in 1645, when, in addition to pulling down part of the nave, they destroyed most of the monastic buildings, in order to use the materials for the erection of guard-houses, and to strengthen the fortifications.

Dr. Todd says: "The Abbey Clois^rs, part of ye Deanery, and Chapter-House.... they pulled down, and employed ye stone to build a maine guard, and a guard-house at every gate; to repair ye walls, and other secular uses as they thought fit."

The **Fratry** still remains. It was built about the middle of the fourteenth century, and rebuilt by Prior Gondibour (1484-1511) towards the close of the fifteenth century. It contains the canons' dining-hall, a fine hall, 79 feet by 27. At the upper end is a beautiful little reader's pulpit, and in the north wall there are two handsome canopied niches. The Perpendicular 74 windows on the south side are very fine specimens; the tracery, however, is modern, but that of the west windows is very old. The late Mr. Street very carefully restored the fratry in 1880, and it is now used as a chapter-house, library, and choir-school. Beneath the fratry is a very fine Decorated crypt, with a groined roof. The boss of one of the pillars bears the initials of Prior Gondibour.

Near the fratry, to the south-west, is the prior's lodging, which, having been enlarged, is now the **Deanery**. It has an embattled tower, and was a refuge for the abbey inmates when danger was near; in fact, to all intents and purposes it was a "peel tower." Formerly there was a covered passage leading from the first floor, over the cloisters, into the cathedral. There is a remarkable room in the deanery, the priors' dining-hall, with a very fine ceiling, put up by Prior Senhouse (1507-1520). It is of oak, richly carved and painted; and covered profusely with verses, armorial bearings, and devices. In every third compartment are two birds holding a scroll between them, on which, and on the cross beams, the following rude verses are written in old English characters: —

> Remember man ye gret pre-emynence,Geven unto ye by God
> omnipotente;Between ye and angels is lytill difference,And
> all thinge erthly to the obediente.By the byrde and beist un-
> der ye fyrmament,Say what excuse mayste thou lay or
> finde;Thus you are made by God so excellenteBut that you
> aughteste again to hy' be kinde,

Sonus sette yis Roofe and Scalope here,
To the intent wythin thys place they shall have prayers every day in
the yere.
Lofe God and thy prynce and you neydis not dreid thy enimys.

The abbey gateway is to the north-west of the nave. It is a plain, round-headed archway, built by Prior Christopher Slee, and bears the following inscription: — "Ora te pʳ anima Christofori Slee Prioris qui primus hoc opus fieri incipit A.D. MDXXVII." Formerly, it was provided with battlements, which have now been removed.

Near the south transept, two arches of the vestibule of the chapter-house are still visible.

Table of
Contents
75

CHAPTER IV

HISTORY OF THE SEE

Ecgfrith, king of Northumbria, drove the Britons away from what is now the northern part of Lancashire, and the Lake district, 670-675. Some years later he granted Carlisle with a circuit of fifteen miles to St. Cuthbert, Bishop of Lindisfarne (685-687), and his successors. In 883 Chester-le-street was chosen as the seat of the bishopric on account of the Northmen's raids on Lindisfarne, and in 995 the see was finally removed to Durham. Carlisle thus formed part of the bishopric of Durham until the death of Flambard in 1128. This bishop had greatly displeased Henry I., and in order to curb the power of the bishops of Durham he reduced the size of the diocese. Carlisle, owing to its distance from Durham, and because of the laxity of ecclesiastical supervision in the surrounding district, was chosen as the seat of a new bishopric, and, with about half of the present counties of Westmoreland and Cumberland, made independent of Durham. A further reason for the choice of Carlisle may have been the presence of the priory church begun by Walter, and finished by Henry I. William Rufus in his lifetime had definitely made the district of Carlisle part of the kingdom of England, and "Henry gave the special care of this last won possession of the English Crown to a prelate, whose name of Æthelwulf is sure proof of his English birth." Æthelwulf, the king's own confessor and prior of Carlisle, was accordingly consecrated bishop in 1133.

More than 400 years later, at the Reformation, the priory was dissolved (1547) and the cathedral re-dedicated to the Holy and Undivided Trinity.

In 1856, on the death of Bishop Percy, a large part of Westmoreland was transferred to Carlisle, and the diocese now embraces all Cumberland (except the parish of Alston), Westmoreland, and Lancashire north of the Sands.

Aldulf (or **Æthelwulf**) (1133-1155), Prior of St. Oswald's (Nostell); Prior of Carlisle; Confessor to Henry I. He 76 was one of those who elected Henry Murdac, Abbot of Fountains Abbey, to the archbishopric of York, although the election displeased Stephen; and received him as his metropolitan when he came to Carlisle on a visit to David, king of Scotland, in 1148. He died in 1155.

Bernard (1203), Archbishop of Ragusa. For more than thirty years there was no appointment made to the see, perhaps because "the bishop's revenues were so small that no able and loyal person would accept thereof." It is not known how long Bernard held the bishopric.

Hugh of Beaulieu (1218-1223), Abbot of Beaulieu, Hampshire, was constituted Bishop of Carlisle by Gualo the Pope's legate. Henry III. had complained to Honorius III. that the canons had elected a bishop against his will and in opposition to the legate, and had sworn fealty to the king of Scotland, at that time the enemy alike of Henry and Honorius. So the canons were banished, and Hugh made bishop. He died at La Ferté, Burgundy, while returning from Rome.

Walter Mauclerk (1223-1246). This bishop was a favourite of King John, and was employed by him on many missions; for instance, in 1215 he was sent to Rome to support the king against the barons; and in 1228 he went on an embassy to Germany to treat for the king's marriage with Leopold of Austria's daughter. He was made treasurer of England by charter in 1232. The following year he was deprived of the office by the machinations of the Bishop of Winchester, and fined £100. Mauclerk set out to appeal to the Pope, but was stopped at Dover by command of the king. The Bishop of London, happening to witness this ill-treatment, excommunicated all those who were hindering Mauclerk, and, proceeding to the king at Hereford, renewed the sentence, in which he was supported by all the bishops there present. This had the effect of gaining permission for the release of Mauclerk, and leave to go to Flanders. In 1234 the bishop was restored to favour. He resigned the bishopric in 1246, and became a Dominican friar at Oxford. When this order of friars first came into England he had stood their friend, presenting them with land and mills. He died in 1248.

Sylvester de Everdon (1247-1255), Archdeacon of Chester; Lord High Chancellor. Sylvester was among the bishops who supported the Archbishop of Canterbury in his 77 opposition to the king's encroachments upon the liberties of the Church, particularly in the matter of electing bishops. He was killed in 1255 by falling from his horse.

Thomas Vipont (1255-1256). This bishop enjoyed the bishopric for less than a year. He died in October 1256.

Two years elapsed before the next appointment.

Robert de Chause (1258-1278), Archdeacon of Bath; Chaplain to Queen Eleanor.

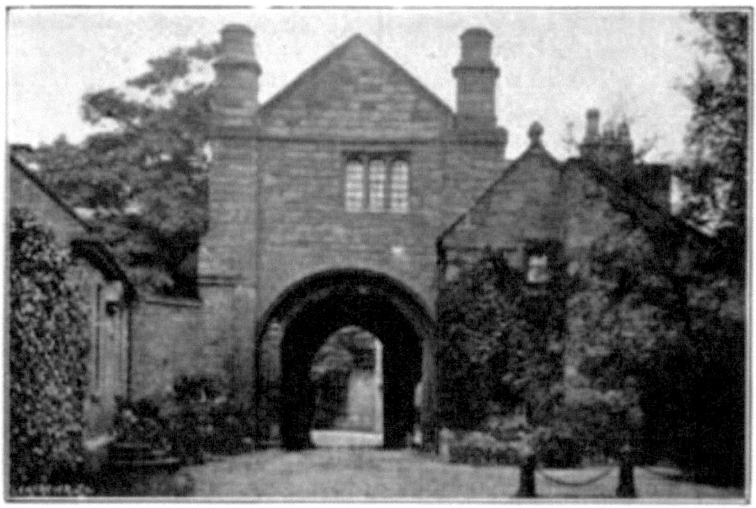

THE ABBEY GATEWAY.

Again there was an interval of two years before the appointment of

Ralph Ireton (1280-1292), Prior of Gisburne. He was elected by the prior and canons of Carlisle, in 1278, without royal licence; so the king (Edward I.) fined the chapter 500 marks, and refused his assent. Eventually Pope Nicholas III. quashed the appointment on the grounds that it had been technically wrong, and then nominated Ireton to the vacant see. Edward agreed to this, pardoned the prior on payment of £100, and restored the temporalities in 1280. Ireton was avaricious, and extorted money from the clergy. This he used 78 for building a new roof to the cathedral. He died in 1292, and was buried in the cathedral; where, shortly after, his tomb and a great deal of his work was destroyed by the great fire which occurred in May that same year.

John of Halton (1292-1324), Canon and Prior of Carlisle; Custos of Carlisle Castle. He defended the city against Wallace. The diocese suffered so often from the ravages of the Scots that more than once he had to obtain remission of the Papal taxation levied on the clergy. He was employed many times in various negotiations with Scotland, his last embassy being in 1320. He died four years later, and was buried in the cathedral.

John de Ros (or **Rosse**) (1325-1332), Canon of Hereford. He was appointed by the Pope to Carlisle in 1325. During his episcopate he was frequently non-resident. He died in 1332.

John de Kirkby (1332-1352), Prior of Carlisle, was bishop during very troubled times, and took part in many raids made on the Scots. He helped to raise the siege of Edinburgh in 1337. Five years later he took part in an expedition to raise the siege of Lochmaben Castle. In 1345 the Scots made a raid into Cumberland, and were defeated. The bishop, while fighting valorously against them, was unhorsed and nearly taken prisoner. The following year he was one of the English leaders at the battle of Neville's Cross. He died in 1352.

Gilbert Welton (1353-1362). The chapter of Carlisle had, with the king's leave, elected John de Horncastle, but the Pope annulled the election, and made Gilbert Welton bishop. He was a very busy official of the king; amongst other matters he was one of the commissioners who treated for the ransom of David of Scotland, and was also a warden of the western marches.

Thomas Appleby (1363-1395), Canon of Carlisle. More than once during his episcopate he was a warden of the western marches. In 1372 he was required by the king, in conjunction with the Bishop of Durham, and others, to be ready to repel any invasion by the Scots. He was also one of the commissioners, in 1384, to treat with the king of Scotland for a renewal of the truce, and, in 1392, to execute that part of a treaty with France which concerned Scottish affairs. He died in 1395.

Robert Reade (1396-1397), a Dominican friar. In 1394 79 he was appointed by the Pope to the bishopric of Waterford and Lismore, and, in spite of the election of William Strickland by the canons, translated to Carlisle, whose temporalities he received in March 1396. In October, however, he was translated (by Papal bull) to Chichester, receiving the temporalities of that see May 1397.

Thomas Merke (or **Merkes**) (1397-1400). Educated at Oxford. The Pope, at the king's request, compelled the chapter of Carlisle to elect him in 1397. He is said to have been a boon companion of Richard II., and remained faithful to that king. He was one of the eight whose safety Richard demanded when surrendering to Bolingbroke. He is said to have made a strong protest in Henry IV.'s first parliament (October 1399) against the treatment which Richard had received. The following January he was tried for high treason, and, after being deprived of his bishopric, was committed to the Abbey of Westminster (23d June 1400). Pope Boniface IX. intervened in his favour, and, by translating him to a titular eastern see *(ad ecclesiam Samastone)*, prevented his being degraded and handed over to the secular arm. He died in 1409, having, after his deposition, held benefices at Sturminster, Marshall, and Todenham, his eastern see affording him no revenue.

William Strickland (1400-1419), whose election (after the death of Bishop Appleby) had been annulled, was now made bishop. He rebuilt the tower of the cathedral, and provided the tabernacle work in the choir. He also furnished Penrith with water from the Petteril. He died in 1419, and was buried in the cathedral.

Roger Whelpdale (1420-1422). Educated at, and Fellow of, Balliol College, Oxford; Provost of Queen's College. He founded and endowed a chantry in the cathedral, and made various bequests to his old colleges at Oxford, dying in London 1422.

William Barrow (1423-1429), Chancellor of the University of Oxford; translated from Bangor. In 1429 he was one of the commissioners for the truce with Scotland which was concluded at Hawden Stank. He died in 1429, and was buried in the cathedral.

Marmaduke Lumley (1430-1450). Educated at Cambridge; Chancellor of the University of Cambridge and Master of Trinity Hall. In 1447 he became Lord High Treasurer of 80 England. Queen's College, Cambridge, was indebted to him for gifts of money towards its building, and books for its library. He was translated to Lincoln in 1450, and died in December of that same year.

Nicholas Close (1450-1452), Fellow of King's College, Cambridge; Chancellor of the University; Archdeacon of Colchester. Translated to the bishopric of Coventry and Lichfield 1452, and died two months after his translation. He was a great benefactor to King's College.

William Percy (1452-1462), Chancellor of the University of Cambridge. Died in 1462.

John Kingscott (1462-1463), Archdeacon of Gloucester.

Richard Scroope (1464-1468), Chancellor of the University of Cambridge.

Edward Story (1468-77), Fellow of Pembroke Hall; Master of Michael House, Cambridge, and Chancellor of the University. He was translated to Chichester 1477.

Richard Bell (1478-1495), Prior of Durham. He died in 1495, and was buried in the choir of the cathedral, where there is a fine brass to his memory.

William Senhouse or **Sever** (1496-1502). Educated at Oxford; Abbot of York. He was one of the commissioners sent to negotiate the marriage of Margaret, daughter of Henry VII., with James IV. Translated to Durham 1502.

Roger Leyburn (1503-1508), Master of Pembroke Hall, Cambridge; Archdeacon of Durham. Died 1508.

John Penny (1509-1520). Educated at Lincoln College, Oxford; Abbot of St. Mary de Pratis, Leicester, 1496; Bishop of Bangor, 1504. Translated to Carlisle 1509. Died in 1520, at Leicester, and was buried there.

John Kite (1521-1537), "a creature of Wolsey." Educated at Eton, and King's College, Cambridge. He was appointed Archbishop of Armagh, by provision of Pope Leo X. 1513, and in 1521 translated to Carlisle. In 1529 he approved the action of Henry VIII. in calling in question his marriage with Catherine of Aragon, and in 1530 he signed the letter to the Pope which demanded Henry's divorce. Four years later he renounced the Pope's supremacy. His epitaph says that during his episcopate he kept "nobyl Houshold wyth grete Hospitality." He died in London 1537, and was buried in Stepney Church.

81**Robert Aldridge** (1537-1556). He was educated at Eton, and King's College, Cambridge. Friend of Erasmus; Registrar of the Order of the Garter; Provost of Eton; and Almoner to Queen Jane Seymour.

Until the close of the year 1550 his opinion was much sought after on questions affecting the Sacrament and the mass, which at that period were much in dispute.

Owen Oglethorpe (1557-1559), Fellow of Magdalen College, Oxford. Living in the troublous times of Henry VIII. and Edward VI. he had, somewhat reluctantly, given his adhesion to the new order and form of service of the holy communion. He was raised to the bishopric of Carlisle by Mary in 1557. The following year she died, and the bishop being called upon to say mass before the new queen, elevated the Host, although she had expressly forbidden it. "A good-natur'd man, and when single by himself very plyable to please Queen Elizabeth," he crowned her queen when the rest of his order refused to perform the ceremony. But "when in conjunction with other Popish Bishops, such principles of stubbornness were distilled into him" that he refused to take the oath of supremacy, and was accordingly deprived of his bishopric the following May. His death, which occurred 31st December 1559, is said to have been hastened by his remorse at having crowned Elizabeth — an enemy of the "true Church" — queen of England.

John Best (1560-1570). After the death of Oglethorpe, the bishopric was offered to "the excellent and pious" Bernard Gilpin, "the apostle of the north," but he refused it.

John Best was then consecrated. He was educated at

Oxford. At the beginning of Queen Mary's reign he had given up all his preferments and lived privately and obscurely. Four years after his consecration he had permission from the queen "to arm himself against the ill-doings of papists and other disaffected persons in his diocese." He died in 1570, and was buried in the cathedral.

Richard Barnes (1570-1577), Fellow of Brasenose College, Oxford; Suffragan-Bishop of Nottingham 1567; translated to Durham 1577. In a letter dated 1576 Barnes alludes to Carlisle as "this poore and bare living."

John Maye (1577-1598), Master of Catherine Hall; Vice-Chancellor of Cambridge. He died in February 1598 while 82 the plague was ravaging Carlisle, and was buried in the cathedral.

Henry Robinson (1598-1616). Educated at Queen's College, Oxford, of which college he became Provost 1581. He took part in the Hampton Court Conference 1603, and was a great benefactor to his college. He died of the plague in 1616, and was buried in the cathedral, where his brother placed a brass to his memory.

Robert Snowden (1616-1621), Prebendary of Southwell. Died 1621.

Richard Milburn (1621-1624), Dean of Rochester. Translated from St. David's. He died 1624.

Richard Senhouse (1624-1626). Educated at Trinity College, and St. John's College, Cambridge. Dean of Gloucester. He preached at the coronation of Charles I. His death, which was caused by a fall from his horse, took place in 1626, and he was buried in the cathedral.

Francis White (1626-1629), Dean of Carlisle; translated to Norwich 1629. He brought himself into notice by preaching against popery; by a book written in antagonism to Fisher, the Jesuit; and, further, by holding a disputation with the same man in the presence of James I.

Barnaby Potter (1629-1642). Educated at, and Provost of Queen's College, Oxford; Chief Almoner of Charles I. Potter was one of the four bishops who advised Charles upon the attainder of Strafford. He died in London 1642.

James Usher (1642-1656). Educated at Trinity College, Dublin; Bishop of Meath; Archbishop of Armagh. He visited England in 1640, and was consulted by the Earl of Strafford in preparing a defence against his impeachment. Charles I. also consulted him as to whether he should sanction the death of the Earl. Usher was present at the execution of Strafford, and ministered to him in his last moments. In 1641 Archbishop Usher suffered severe losses from a rebellion in Ireland; and this is no doubt the reason why he never returned to that country. About this time Charles I. gave him the bishopric of Carlisle *in commendam*, but the Archbishop does not seem to have obtained much revenue therefrom, as the district was greatly impoverished through the English and Scottish troops being alternately quartered there. A few years later Parliament seized on his lands and voted him an annual pension of £400, which, however, he probably did not receive more than twice. During the troubles of these times he resided at Oxford and Cardiff. He came to London in 1646, and the next year, through his friend's endeavours, he was allowed to preach. He visited Charles at Carisbrooke in 1648. He died in 1656, and was buried, by order of Cromwell, in Westminster Abbey. He wrote "On the Original State of the British Churches," "The Ancient History of the British Churches," and his great work on sacred chronology, "The Annals of the Old Testament." It is said that Baxter wrote his famous "Call to the Unconverted" at the Archbishop's suggestion.83

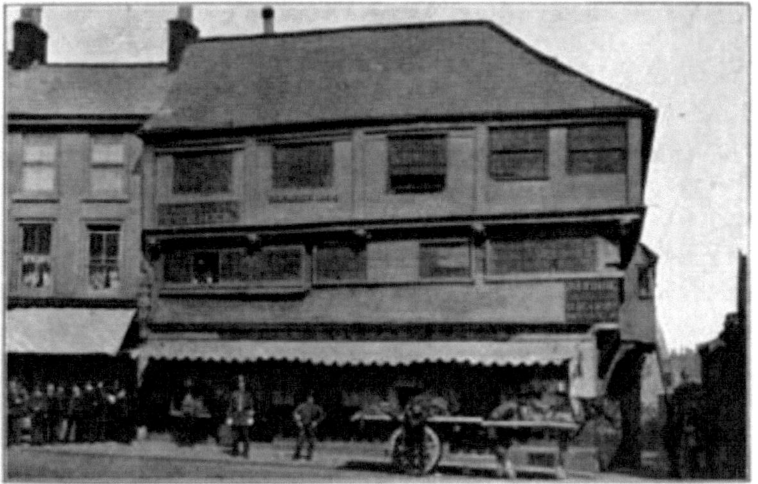

REDNESS HALL.

85**Richard Sterne** (1660-1664). Educated at Trinity College; Master of Jesus College, Cambridge. He sided with the king on the outbreak of civil war, and was arrested by Cromwell in 1642 for endeavouring to send the college plate to Charles, and imprisoned in the Tower till the January following. He was kept prisoner in various places until 1645. He regained his Mastership at the Restoration, and soon after was made Bishop of Carlisle. He was translated to the archbishopric of York, leaving his bishopric in a very impoverished state. Sterne the novelist was his great-grandson.

Edward Rainbow (1664-1684). Educated at Corpus Christi College, Oxford, and Magdalene College, Cambridge; he became Master of the latter in 1642-3. Dean of Peterborough 1661. He was very hospitable and liberal. He did not hesitate in years of scarcity (after he had exhausted his own stores of provisions) to buy corn which he gave away to the poor day by day. He died in 1684, and was buried at Dalston.

Thomas Smith (1684-1702). Educated at Queen's College; Prebendary of Durham; Dean of Carlisle. He was a very generous benefactor to Queen's College, Oxford, the Carlisle Grammar School, the chapter library, and the cathedral treasury. He died in 1702.

William Nicolson (1702-1718). A very learned antiquary. Fellow of Queen's College, Oxford, and Archdeacon of Carlisle. His most noted work is the "Historical Library" (1696-1699), which at one time "afforded a guide to the riches of the chronicle literature of the British empire." He was translated to the bishopric of Derry in 1718.

86**Samuel Bradford** (1718-1723). Educated at St. Paul's School, the Charterhouse, and Corpus Christi, Cambridge. He was elected Master of Corpus Christi College in 1716. Dean of Westminster. Translated to Rochester 1723.

John Waugh (1723-1734). Educated at, and Fellow of Queen's College, Oxford; Dean of Gloucester. Died 1734.

Sir George Fleming, Bart. (1735-1747). Educated at St. Edmund Hall, Oxford; Dean of Carlisle. During his episcopate the Young Pretender entered Carlisle (1745) and it is said that he installed one Thomas Coppock, or Cappoch, a Roman Catholic, as bishop. Coppock was captured, and executed at Carlisle the following year. Sir George Fleming died in 1747, and was buried in the cathedral.

Richard Osbaldeston (1747-1762). Educated at St. John's College, Cambridge; Dean of York. He was chiefly a non-resident bishop, and, on his translation to London in 1762, his successor complained bitterly of the state of dilapidation and decay into which Rose Castle, the bishop's residence, had been allowed to fall.

Charles Lyttelton (1762-1768). Educated at Eton, and University College, Oxford; Dean of Exeter. In 1765 he was president of the Society of Antiquaries. He wrote numerous articles, some of which are included in the first three volumes of the "Archæologia." He was very genial and hospitable, and had a remarkable knowledge of antiquities. He died in London 1768, and was buried at Hagley.

Edmund Law (1769-1787). Educated at St. John's College, Cambridge; Fellow of Christ's College. He was an earnest student, and zealous for Christian truth and Christian liberty. He believed that the human race progresses in religion equally with its progress in all other knowledge. He is said to have been "a man of great softness of manners, and of the mildest and most tranquil disposition." He died in 1787, and was buried in the cathedral.

John Douglas (1787-1791). Educated at St. Mary Hall, Oxford, and Balliol; Dean of Windsor; translated to Salisbury 1791. He wrote many political pamphlets.

The Hon. Edward Venables Vernon (1791-1808), Canon of Christ Church, Oxford; translated to York 1808. He assumed the name of Harcourt in 1831.

Samuel Goodenough (1808-1827). Educated at Westminster, 87 and Christ Church, Oxford; Canon of Windsor, and Dean of Rochester.

In 1809 a sermon preached before the House of Lords gave rise to the following epigram: —

> 'Tis well enough that Goodenough
> Before the Lords should preach; But, sure enough, full bad enough
> Are those he has to teach.

He died in 1827, and was buried in Westminster Abbey.

Hugh Percy (1827-1856). Educated at Trinity College, Cambridge; Bishop of Rochester, whence he was translated to Carlisle. During his episcopate he established a Clergy Aid Society (1838), and a Diocesan Education Society (1855). He died in 1856, and was buried at Dalston.

Henry Montague Villiers (1856-1860). Translated to Durham 1860.

Samuel Waldegrave (1860-1869). Educated at Oxford; Canon of Salisbury. Author of "New Testament Millenarianism" (the Bampton Lectures, 1854). Died 1869.

Harvey Goodwin (1869-1891). Second Wrangler, Cambridge; Dean of Ely. A very politic bishop. In one of his sermons he used words to the effect that "he was as high as the church was high, as low as the church was low, and as broad as the church was broad." Died 1891.

J.W. Bardsley (1892). Translated from Sodor and Man.88

LIST OF PRIORS AND DEANS

PRIORS

Æthelwulf (Aldulf)	Galfrid
Walter	John de Horncastle (resigned 1376)
John	Thomas Hextildsham
Bartholomew	Richard de Rydale
Ralph	John de Penrith (resigned 1381)
Robert Morville	William de Dalston
Adam de Felton	Robert de Edenhall. 1386
Alan	Thomas de Hoton
John Halton (Bishop, 1292)	Thomas Elye
John Kendall	Thomas Barnaby. 1433
Robert	Thomas de Haythwaite
Adam Warthwic (resigned 1304)	Thomas Gondibour. 1484-1507
	Simon Senhouse. 1507
William Hautwyssel	Christopher Slee
Robert Helperton	Lancelot Salkeld. 1532. (Last Prior and
Simon Hautwyssel (about	1st Dean)

1325)
William de Hastworth.
1325
John Kirby (Bishop, 1332)

DEANS

Lancelot Salkeld. 1542
Sir Thomas Smyth, LL. D. 1547
Lancelot Salkeld. 1553.
Sir Thomas Smyth, LL.D. 1559
Sir John Wooley, M.A. 1577
Christopher Perkins, LL.D. 1596
Francis White, S.T.P. 1622
William Patterson, S.T.P. 1626
Thomas Comber S.T.P 1630
   (Vacant 18 years)
Guy Carleton, D.D. 1660
Thomas Smith, D.D. 1671
Thomas Musgrave, D.D. 1684
William Graham, D.D. 1686
Francis Atterbury, D.D. 1704
George Smallridge, D.D. 1711
Thomas Gibbon, D.D. 1713

Thomas Tullie, LL.D. 1716
George Fleming, LL.D. 1727
Robert Bolton, LL.D. 1734
Charles Tarrent, D.D. 1764
Thomas Wilson, D.D. 1764
Thomas Percy, D.D. 1778
Jeffrey Ekins, D.D. 1782
Isaac Milner, D.D. 1792
Robert Hodgson, D.D. 1820
John Anthony Cramer, D.D. 1844
Samuel Hinds, D.D. 1848
Archibald Campbell Tait, D.D. 1849
Francis Close, D.D. 1856
J. Oakley, D.D. 1881
W.G. Henderson, D.D. 1884

CHAPTER V

THE CASTLE

The **Castle** is built on the highest ground in the city, a kind of cliff at the north-west angle rising abruptly about sixty feet above the river Eden. An area of nearly three acres has been enclosed with walls, the longest side from north-west to south-east being about 256 yards long, the west side 143 yards, and the south side 200 yards. Two sides are very steep, and the south side, which slopes gradually to the town, is defended outside the wall by a wide moat 10 feet deep.

There are two divisions: the outer ward, and the inner ward. William Rufus erected the keep, which was at first the only building on the site, and this was enclosed by a wall on the north and east. A triangular ward was thus formed, having its entrance at the south-east. Carlisle was fortified in 1170, and the city walls were carried up to the castle. At this time the first entrance was blocked up and the present one made; the outer ward was also enclosed. The south wall, with its flat buttresses, is partly Norman, and partly thir-teenth-century work; and this description generally applies to the north and west walls.

About 50 yards from the south-west angle and on the city walls is King Richard's Tower, a building of two storeys, where Richard III. is said to have lived when at Carlisle. It is also called the Tile Tower because of the thin bricks with which it was built. A subterranean passage leading to the keep was discovered here early this century. Entrance to the castle is gained by a bridge crossing the moat; this has replaced the old drawbridge and leads to a gatehouse with bat-tlements, a kind of barbican, of two storeys. The passage is vaulted, and has massive doors of oak studded with iron; formerly there was also a portcullis.

This leads to the outer ward which is about four times as large as the inner ward. It is nearly square, and contains modern buildings for the use of the garrison.

90 The two wards are divided by a strong stone wall 90 yards in length. A wide ditch (now filled up) once ran in front. In the centre

of this wall is a building — the Captain's Tower — which gives access to the inner ward through its gateway secured at each end with a strong door.

Some of the masonry of the Captain's Tower is Norman, but it is mostly Decorated. A half-moon battery of three guns once defended the Tower and commanded the outer ward, but it has now been removed.

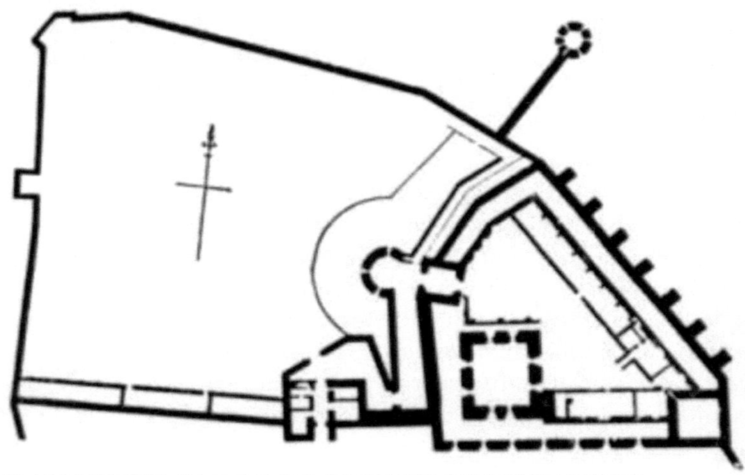

PLAN OF THE CASTLE (TIME OF QUEEN ELIZABETH).

The inner ward contains the great square keep, 66 feet by 61, where the governor had his apartments, and which was the final resort of the garrison when the place was entered by an enemy. The walls are 15 feet in thickness, except on the east side, which is only 8 feet thick. The building consists of a basement and three upper floors; the highest floor is vaulted to sustain a platform for artillery. The present height is 68 feet. On a clear day a fine view can be had from the top, embracing the mountains in the Lake district, the heights of Northumberland, the Solway Firth, and the Scottish coast. Several cells have been contrived in the eastern wall, in one of which Major McDonald (Fergus McIvor) is said to have 91 been lodged. Some of the cell walls have been carved at various times with figures of men, birds, and animals. These were, perhaps, executed with a nail. In the north wall is the shaft of a well, 78 feet deep. This is supposed to be the well which was shown to St. Cuthbert when he visited Carlisle. The dungeons are in the ground floor, and of course are distinguished by a plentiful lack of daylight and fresh air.

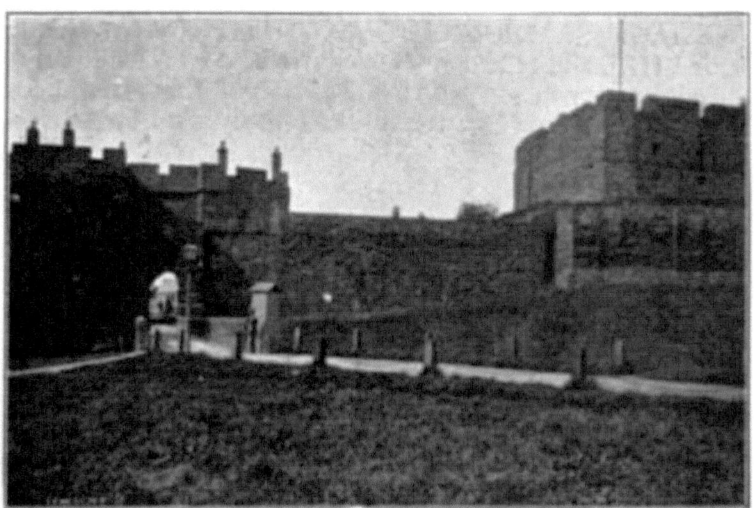

THE CASTLE.

Queen Mary's Tower, so called from having been the prison of Mary Queen of Scots, was in the south-east angle of the inner ward. It was pulled down in 1835, and a wall built round the angle. It was in part Norman work of the time of William Rufus, and partly Early English; and had a large rounded archway springing from capitals with zigzag decoration. There was also a portcullis for its defence. A passage used by Queen Mary to pass out to the Lady's Walk, which ran eastward from the gatehouse, has been walled up.

The Long Hall, a fine structure about 100 feet by 40, in which the Parliament of 1306-7 met, was also situated in this ward, but was demolished with several other buildings, 1824-1835. 92 At various times the castle has undergone extensive repairs, notably in the reigns of Richard III., Edward III., Henry VIII., and Elizabeth.

During the siege in 1644-5 it suffered much damage, and was patched up by the Parliamentary troops. A hundred years later the

Duke of Cumberland thought very little of its powers of defence, for he contemptuously called it "an old hen-coop."

Among the governors, several well-known men figure; for instance, Andrew Harcla, the Duke of Gloucester (afterwards Richard III.), and Hotspur. Upon the death of Lieutenant-General Ramsay in 1837 the office of governor was abolished. The castle now furnishes barrack accommodation for troops, and serves as a depôt.

DIMENSIONS OF CARLISLE CATHEDRAL

Choir, Length	134 feet
Choir, Breadth	72 feet
Choir, Height	72 feet
Nave, Length	39 feet
Nave, Breadth	60 feet
Nave, Height	65 feet
Transepts, Length	124 feet
Transepts, Breadth	28 feet
Tower, Height	112 feet
AREA	15,270 sq. ft.

93

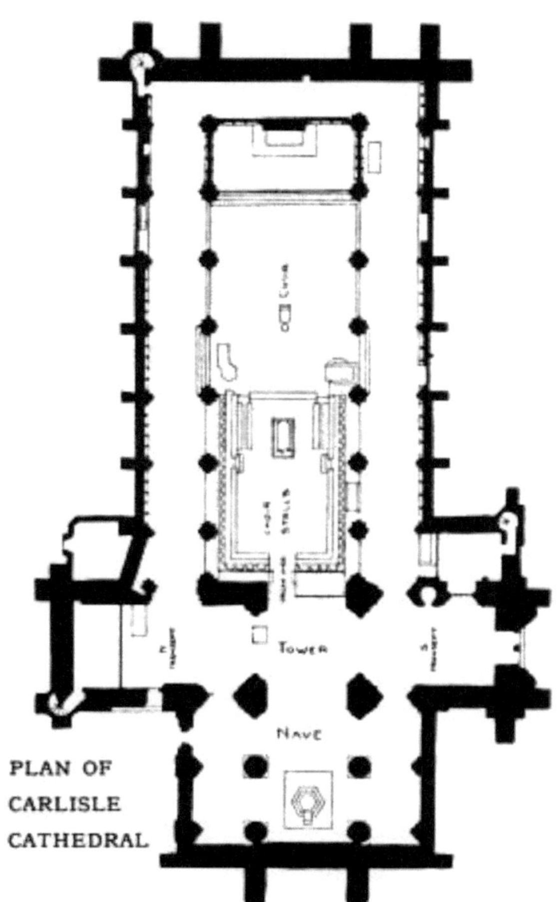

PLAN OF CARLISLE CATHEDRAL

FOOTNOTES

[1] Nicholson and Burn, page 249.

[2] These date from about 1400.

[3] "History of Carlisle," page 158.

[4] "Guide to the Cathedral of Carlisle," by R.H. and K.H.

[5] Jefferson, "History of Carlisle," p. 180.

[6] "Guide to the Cathedral of Carlisle," by R.H. and K.H.